Giving Up
the Ghost

Giving Up the Ghost

Let Go Of Grief and Restore Your Life

Karen Schultz

To order additional copies of this book, contact:
Xlibris LLC
1-888-795-4274
www.Xlibris.com
Orders@Xlibris.com
549500

Contents

Acknowledgments

To my husband Rick Schultz, without his love and support, I would not have my business. He has always been there for me, and I am so grateful to have him. He lost his father at a young age. He told me that people grieve differently, and to respect each person's choice in this regard. I finally got what he said!

To my children Carlos and Sarah Schultz, for their honesty and sense of humor. They are lights in my life, and I am happy God entrusted us with them. May they have long and fruitful lives. And may God give me strength!

To my rabbi guides, who have brought me out of sorrow into the light. To the ones who make me laugh and tell me what my purpose is. May these angels of light continue to guide me on my spiritual path. To Rabbi Nachman of Breslov who taught me how to turn loss into love, and how to never give up. His spirit helped me to heal depression and loss in my own life. Thank you for showing up!

To Marlene Waldner, who always encouraged me to be more productive and to love myself. Her loving care and compassion have strengthened me and my soul. Thank you for all the years of support and wisdom. You are an inspiration to me, to your family as well as to your clients. Thanks for all the tapes, articles, and other resources you have given me. You are very kind to me. I appreciate all of your efforts. You are an angel on earth!

To my consultant Nancy Ging, she is the example of what healing is. She has a soul that is both deep and alive. She never tells me what to do but urges my higher self to do the right thing. She has so many energetic connections from countless healing spaces and places. May she continue on in her quest to heal herself, her clients, and the planet.

Thanks for writing the foreword to this book. You may reach Nancy at www.nancyging.com.

To John Adolf and the Adolph Funeral Home staff especially Donna, Barb, Christine, Karen, and Bob; and to Tony Adolf who has passed from this world, and his wife Irene and family, thank you for allowing me to be part of an amazing group of people committed to outstanding service to others in their time of need and for offering group support services to those families that enter through your door.

To Dr. John Canine and Shirley Brogan of Maximum Living Consultants, thank you for the opportunity to work with the Adolph Family, and for your help and guidance with the support groups at the funeral home. I admire your dedication to those who are grieving. Your organization helps many families in need.

To Cindi Muntz, spiritual medium who does great work connecting the other side with earth, thank you for doing the workshop and for your support of clients we may have in common. You are real and always honest. I wish you continued prosperity in all of your endeavors with the spirit world. You give hope, information, and closure to many people who feel lost after the death of a loved one. Wish you the best with your show on the Bio channel. You may reach Cindi at her website www.cindimuntz.com. She is on Facebook too.

To Lynne Beumer of "heavenly conversations." She is a spiritual channeler. Thanks for telling me about the lipstick I need to wear to church. She has the confidence and ability to speak frankly to everyone. Thanks for being a great friend, and thanks for the readings. You and your daughter Leslie from the other side are a light for this world. You may contact Lynne at (708) 704-4010 for an appointment.

To Lin Bresnahan, a very warm, professional, and smart woman. Thanks for always being a friend and for helping my daughter Sarah. Thanks for letting me use Erik's letter from heaven as proof of life after death. Also, thanks for all the Starbucks for Sarah! I wish you love and a healthy, happy, and long life.

To Gail Galivan of Inner Alchemy, thank you for your healing Qi gong exercises and for your gift of helping people heal physical issues. You are a wonderful person and teacher. Thanks for all of your calmness and help with Carlos. You can reach Gail at (708) 903-7346.

To Anne Quigley, my Reiki teacher and massage therapist, thanks for speaking at my psychic development classes and for your special knowledge of Reiki. Can't wait for my next attunement. This lady is the real deal. You can reach her at anne@pureharmonymassage.com

To Dr. John Mostrando, Chiropractic Physician. Thank you for your kindness and expertise in treating myself and my son Carlos. I appreciate you sharing your vast understanding of the human body, muscles and tips on how to heal. I admire your hard work and dedication to your profession. Thank you for supporting my practice as well. You are a spiritual mentor to our family. We wish you continued prosperity. Thanks for those special pictures from Sedona.

To Denise and Rich Jandura, for hanging in there and creating a life together. Can't forget baby Muffy. You are a dog lover, a five-time cancer survivor, and an incredibly strong woman. You taught me what a spiritual life is all about. You help others, get involved, and have a winning personality and wit. I bless you and Rich, and pray for you both. You are an inspiration to me and to anyone who recovers fully from five different cancers!

To all my clients, group participants, and students who have taken my grief and psychic development classes. You have given me something I will never forget. You make me smile and validate for me that we need more questioning and conversations about death and life. You have all taught me that love never dies, and yet healing does occur if we allow ourselves to open our heart and listen to our soul. Thank you for letting me tell your stories and for sharing.

To the Kabbalah Centers all over the world, your words have given me purpose. Scanning the letters create a fire deep inside me that is alive. This is a powerful tool that will change your life. I am grateful for all of the love and support I have gleaned from tapes, books, meditations, audio, and online. Special mention to Rabbi Yehuda Grundman, who first empowered me to move toward the light and away from fear. Thank you for helping me continue on my spiritual journey. You can reach the Kabbalah Centre by calling 1-800-KABBALAH.

To my mother and father Laura and Eugene Squeri and my deceased brother Michael, I can see how much loss we all had in our lives. I always tried to pretend that all was well when it wasn't. So sorry for your difficult lives, and I hope you are all at peace. May you look down at me and believe that I would do anything to see you all again. I love and accept myself and can now see the strength that you had just by being a survivor, and taking each day one by one. Love you always.

To my living brother James Squeri, I will always help you and keep you safe. I accept that you are doing the best you can. Love you always.

To my cousins Lenore and her daughter Samantha, thanks for all the laughs, support, and friendship. It is nice seeing us the way we were when we were growing up, and now that we are both mothers! We are survivors!

To psychic Sylvia Browne, who was a very big part of my introduction into the spirit world. I know she has passed from this world, but she was a force on Montel and in her books. I admire her honesty and confidence. May she rest in the spirit. She was a pioneer for other women psychics and mediums. She is greatly missed by all she came into contact with. How did she find time to write all those books?

Foreword

With an attitude of gratitude I share some words about this wonderful, practical, and spiritually inspired book. *Giving Up the Ghost* gets my attention for certain. *Let Go of Grief and Restore Your Life* is a directive we all need, as is the wise guidance of this book.

Karen R. Schultz, LCSW, is a colleague for whom I have great respect and admiration. Her compassion, wisdom, and vitality are exceptional. These energies come through the pages of this book. The author shares intimate stories of loss and allows the reader in on the process of what is often needed to get beyond these losses. We are left with hope as we move through this book.

The author has had an exceptional life and, along the way, realized she has a unique guidance system available to her. Her gifts of the spirit and great intuitive abilities allow her to be a profound teacher and comforter. I once heard a clergyperson say, "We are not here to be comfortable; we are here to be comforters." Karen Schultz can bring readers, uncomfortable in their grief and pain, to a place of greater comfort.

An expanded world view comes to the reader in the process of reading this book. It informs us on many levels as it is about energy. As we move into the process of letting go of grief and restoring our lives, we move from the contracted, condensed energy of pain into the expanded and enlivening energy of Light and Spirit. As we move into what I have called "the energy paradigm" in my first book, we can bring balance to our lives, letting the world of subtle energies and Spirit support us in the process of living with our often energetically dense and painful human condition.

Unresolved grief can do more damage than bring us emotional discomfort. If we do not learn how to let it go, we can become physically ill. This book supports the reader in connecting with levels of truth which can make a significant difference, offering us peace and practical behavioral steps, such as building community and finding group support. In our lives, we are called to do what we cannot do alone. Help abounds, both within the world of spirit and among people we meet along the way. As this author tells us, "We are angels with one wing and we need to embrace each other." With joy I embrace this book.

Nancy B. Ging, LCSW
Holistic psychotherapist and author of *Simplifying the Road to Wholeness*
www.nancyging.com

Chapter 1

Grief in Our Society

Every time I turn around, I am connecting with people who have had a recent loss of a loved one. I always sit next to the person who lost someone at the airport, on a plane, at Disneyland waiting for a ride, and whenever I meet people. Many times I feel like the ambassador for the dead. I am told to carry angels for people when I travel. It happens all the time. My rabbi spirit guides always remind me that while I am at the airport, I am not busy, so why shouldn't I be of service? I am always surprised how random this seems, but it never is. It is always miraculous when people receive the messages from me that their loved ones are in heaven and doing fine. I have yet to be told that someone who passed is in hell. I guess I am lucky in this respect.

My way of giving service to God is by doing what my guides ask of me. I have had many losses in my life, so they say we teach what we most need to learn. I will get phone numbers of certain people in my mind who need my call. I also see faces in my mind. I know this is a gift, but it does take some getting used to. I make phone calls to people who might want to join our support groups. Many times I never get a call back. It doesn't matter, I am compelled to do this work with grieving people. I used to be so afraid of death. I have been a licensed clinical social worker for over thirty years now. I have heard how grief is never discussed in most families.

One man was with his wife since high school, and they never discussed her wishes of what she wanted when she passed. She died in her seventies. This is not uncommon. I have heard from bereaved parents how the community stayed away from their families and how lost and isolated they felt. These stories always surprised me. One lady from my daughter's school spoke to me once about her mom's death, and then never spoke to me again. When I tell people that I support grief education, they always give me a strange look. The secretive nature and fear about the mystery of death always concerned me. These days, young people are just dying out of nowhere. These are people in their twenties and thirties. No explanation is given, and parents are left in shock and horror. These people were so healthy, so alive. How can they be gone so soon?

There is a saying that I find is a metaphor for our lives. It says, "We are all angels with one wing. We need to embrace each other to fly." For many years, I have tried time and again to do everything myself. I have been to the twelve-step meetings, and heard that "together we can do more than we ever could alone." I learned how to look upward and inward but also to connect with others on the recovery road. I hope that this book can shed some light on the process of removing darkness, depression, and despair from one's life. I know about darkness and how it manifests. I have lived in the shadow of myself and have surrounded myself with walls, barriers, and used weight as a protection from the outside world. Whenever I would catch a glimpse of light, I would literally cover my eyes thinking, "It's too bright, it's too bright."

What was I afraid of and why? My whole life I have been afraid of the light because it exposed my flaws and defects of character. I really thought people would see the black holes inside of me. If anyone saw the "real" me, they would run like the wind far away. I never thought that the darkness also hid my strengths and my connection to God. You really can find things in the darkness that can be illuminated by the light. This journey has also been called "the dark night of the soul" by many mystics and monks, as well as new age authors and teachers. One of my main goals with this book is to teach people not to be afraid of the dark. If we look inside ourselves, we often find hidden joy and light in the dark, not only secrets and shame.

Our culture is afraid of loss and grief, and we rarely talk about the loss, making our recovery harder and more challenging. We lack a common language to discuss loss and grief. In fact, people often run away if anyone talks about the death of a family member or friend. It has been my experience that people have avoided me when I try to offer my time or attention to address their loss.

I have spoken to bereaved parents who lost businesses and all contact with friends and employers after the tragic death of one of their children. These people never spoke to my clients, and they felt shunned. One man lost his twenty-two-year-old son, his son's twenty-two-year-old girlfriend, his business, and the support of the community. Another friend had her young daughter die, and neighbors wouldn't talk to her, making the loss all the more painful. People think they would lose their child if they got close enough to the grieving family. Others think they can "catch" something if they venture too close.

I understand the fear and avoidance. It's human to want to stay away from pain. It's our denial system that protects us until we can deal with it—or we are afraid that if we feel anything, we will not function in the world. As part of my job at a local funeral home, I call each family that has their funeral there and ask if they would like to join our grief support group. We also send them a book about grief in the mail to offer them solace. Even though I may call months later after the funeral, it's hard for the family to even talk to us again.

I am writing this book because there is so much trauma and pain that comes from the death process. No one knows how to deal with the medical system in regard to health care for the dying. People know about hospice, but my clients didn't know what a living will was, or how to advocate for their loved one once they are in a nursing home or even at the hospital. I have heard the guilt and shame some of my clients talk about because they didn't get clear messages about their loved one. Even in the case of my own mother, I didn't think that having a low pulse rate could lead to death.

My mom was in New York, and I was in Chicago. Talking to a nurse about her care gave me no insight into what was really happening with her. After I spoke with one nurse, I was alarmed and called back to get clarification on what was going on. The nurse said she wasn't allowed to talk with me more than once, and to call back the next day.

If I knew how close to death she was, I would have hopped on a plane that night. I was taken by surprise with a phone call from the doctor a few days later. Basically he told me that she had too many things wrong with her. He said they worked on her all night and that she was ready to die. He asked who else he had to notify about her impending death. I was floored. I got to go to New York the next day. I was anxious and fearful. She died before I got there.

My dad was there and he knew she was dead. He said, "Maybe she's not really dead." I could see her in the morgue. She had died in the afternoon. I felt so guilty that I wasn't there. My dad's denial was evident and so was mine. I refused to see her in the morgue. I am a sensitive person who would remember the scene and be traumatized by it. No, I said, I would wait until the wake to see her. No one from the hospital spoke to us at all. Once her body was gone from the hospital bed, we had no contact with the doctor.

Something is wrong with the system because these should be times we rally around people and help them with the transition. If they die in the hospital, there should be someone who could comfort them at the time of death.

One of my clients had been married to his wife for forty-one years. He held her as she passed on. He was left alone in the room and had to leave. He visited her every day for four years. Day after day he was at the cemetery. Here is the miracle: There was a funeral home connected with the cemetery. He went there every day and had coffee with the people there. He had his own cup, and they celebrated his birthday there too. They were wonderful to him. It is this kind of loving kindness that feeds the soul.

By far, the most helpful sentence is the one that says, "It is all right if you go home to heaven." Some people need permission to leave this earth. One man heard his daughter tell him that it was all right to leave. He popped open one eye and said, "Really?" She said yes, and he made his way through the doorway of death into heaven. His wife had passed years ago, and he wanted to be with her.

This was a man who knew that he was mean to his wife while she was on earth. He was in our grief support group for over five years trying to make amends for his behavior. He had been to talking to religious people, and shared with the group his sorrow and pain about not being a good husband. He even got her slippers for the bedroom so her feet wouldn't be cold. He wasn't crazy, because he was very serious about making things up to her.

People don't know what to do after a wake and funeral. They feel vulnerable and emotionally open. They figure it's better to leave the family alone. They seem afraid to upset the person by bringing up the deceased once the public funeral is over. Please do not leave the family alone because you are scared. Ask them how they are, and listen when they tell you. Ask them out or offer to take them somewhere. Ask how you can help and then do so.

One client said she would never call and ask something of a neighbor. She preferred that they simply call her and tell her, "We are going out for coffee." Grieving people need to move and get out of the house. Friends need to be more assertive and proactive. Call and say, "What are you doing now? Let's go!"

People feel the loss of community support after the funeral. They think it will always be there, but many times it disappears. This is the time for a support group, counseling, or when good friends just plan fun things. I know that the people who go out regularly with friends and have a social life are the ones that heal the quickest. Remember that we can respond with fear or with love to these people. Very few people actually call you up and ask you to help. Don't abandon them when they have no one to talk to.

Some people have spent years with a cancer patient or with a terminal illness. They are the perfect spouses. They go to every doctor's appointment with their loved one, put on a happy face for the world and never get to meet their own needs during this time. It could last for years. Sometimes the ill person doesn't say thank you to the spouse, or they never tell them that they love them. Some have dementia and may not be nice to their loved ones. Some were mean and angry at their children (adult and child alike), and fought with each other. The relatives feel like that was really them.

It could have been them on some medications, some with dementia, and some that were deathly afraid of the dying process. Many people get angry when they are scared. This can be seen more with men. However, many of my group members blame themselves for the behavior. Please realize that it was not them; it might have been the illness talking. The way they are at the end is not something to hold on to. Forgive them for acting out, cursing, or for any angry outbursts. Many times they don't know how they are acting. Just don't blame yourself for creating behavior that is not in your control.

This stress takes its toll because either the terminal person may not have the brain function they had before the disease, or the treatments like chemotherapy and radiation take its toll on the body and mind of the patient. Many people who are the caretaker for their loved one cry and scream because they wonder what they did it for. Please have compassion for those people who dealt with a progressive disease. They are probably exhausted, sleep deprived, feeling guilty, and just worn out. Some people literally go on for three or four years in the crisis mode. They had the horror of seeing the decline of their loved one little by little. One lady whose husband died from Multiple Sclerosis watched his functions slow down until he could only move a finger.

The trauma of death is real. These people are also parents, and the kids also see the decline. The spouse may be only in their forties or fifties with teenagers and young children to raise. Most of the single dads out there wonder how they are going to live without their spouse. They are torn because they would like to remarry but feel guilty for wanting another partner. Some couples did talk about it and say that they would want their partner to be remarried after their death. Still, it is very hard to date when dealing with the death of a spouse and raising young and teenage children.

As you can see, there are many issues that arise because of a loss. I know one eighteen-year-old girl who lost her mom first, then dad, and then she went to live with her grandmother. The grandmother died and now she is living with aunts and uncles. Will she ever recover? Does she think it's her fault that they died? All these questions cannot be answered. She may also feel abandoned and alone. Who can she turn to for help? Therapists make wonderful mentors to these teens and young adults. Also, a trusted friend can help people with multiple losses.

Sudden deaths are not easy to deal with. Many of these deaths involve teenagers and young adults. Car crashes and cancer have taken many young adults. I have seen a new trend with sudden deaths taking more people than ever. Some perfectly healthy people die while running or playing soccer. Some that die have undiagnosed heart problems. However, some have no heart problems.

These kinds of death shock us and keep us wondering why we lose people at twenty-two or twenty-six or thirty. It is harder to heal from because they truly do not know what happened and why their loved ones died. They are angry sometimes, asking God how he could take their wonderful son when there are bad people doing bad things who get to stay alive. I have no answer for that. Some people agonize over that fact. They think they are being punished for wrongdoing in their own life. Having faith can help, but it still doesn't seem fair.

Some deaths are also difficult because a mother and father bury their child before themselves. Their son or daughter was all that they had. They were there to help their kids. They were like friends.

Some people have died several times before and were able to come back to life. At those times, the adult child was always right there. The mother can't figure out why God didn't take her when she was clinically dead. It may be hard to start a new life because their child was more than just their child. They were like twins. They were companions and did everything together. Who can she trust now? How does she start a new life? Does she even want a new life?

I have been dealing with death for years. I know that the trends are disturbing. Drugs and suicides have risen with no explanations. Have our lives become a pain-filled reminder that our lost loved ones died in a violent, drug- or alcohol-related way? While reading this book, try to understand that it's the people on earth who are suffering. The ones on the other side no longer worry about themselves. Most of the deaths are traumatic in some way, and sometimes hope is overrated. No one can bring back these lost loved ones. That fact is very hard to accept.

My own brother was ripped from our family by a hit-and-run driver. My dad called his death "a dirty trick" from God. He was so angry at God that he turned around all of the religious statues in his house. He felt betrayed and was very angry that his forty-year-old son was taken in such a brutal and violent way. He also wondered what he had done to have this happen to my brother. We simply had to let him express this anger at God for as long as he needed to feel it.

My brother's death was a tragic end to a tragic situation. He was mentally ill and was never able to have a wife and a family. He went to California to find his "niche" in life. The investigators did not think my dad had a case in finding the person who had hit him. They did little to nothing because my brother didn't have a family. This was very hard to take. It was my father's nightmare.

What we can do is to remember what they taught us while they were on earth, and how we can honor them and help others heal. A friend who lost her son went to a support group, and while she was there, she met two other people struggling to find peace and hope. They all helped each other that night. She says that she did not get their names or phone numbers, but each of them exchanged hope with each other. They hugged and cried. They told their stories to one another. Just by opening themselves to the healing quality of a grief support group, they lived another day with the terrible news they did not want. They all walk the same road. It is hard to put one foot in front of the other when everything turns to chaos and anxiety.

We can share with others and have compassion for those who are wounded, destroyed, and devastated by the death of a loved one. Be loving to them and help them to accept the "new normal" or life without their loved one. We can let go of fear and know that, for some people, their loved ones can help them more in heaven than they ever could while they were alive. This book shares how a grief community can be a soothing and healing balm for the members. Together we can do more than we can ever do alone.

When I was eight, my grandpa died. He lived with my grandmother in Brooklyn, New York. They lived next door to a Jewish Orthodox Synagogue. I was interested in what went on there. I would peek out of the window and talk with the girl who lived there. Once she told me that no women were allowed in the synagogue. I was always happy that God lived next door to my grandparents.

My grandfather and grandmother migrated to the United States from Italy. They worked very hard each day in the garment industry of New York. It was a hard and somewhat dangerous job, as grandmother always put her money in her bra to conceal how much she had. I remember eating at a place called the "automat." There were vending machines in a big room where you could purchase different kinds of food. The city was cool to me, but the trains ran all night long.

My grandparents were in an arranged marriage. My grandfather was very mad because my grandmother had some severe psychiatric issues he was not told about. That's why they only had one child. My mother was brought up with cousins and relatives around her. My grandmother and grandfather always worked very hard for their money. Grandmother was hospitalized several times when my mom was young.

When they came to visit us on Long Island, they slept in different rooms. My grandfather called me into his room one night and pointed to a table beside the bed he was sleeping in. He asked me to take down the table for him the next day. I thought that was odd, but I said "sure." I was the last person to see him before he died. That night, the cat was making a moaning sound, and it woke me up. My grandmother was sleeping with me in the double bed.

The next thing I know was that I hear my mother screaming, "Papa! Papa! No! It can't be true!" She ran up the stairs and found him dead. I remember he died on the day they buried John Kennedy after he was shot and killed. What had happened was that my grandmother got up and went downstairs to get coffee. My mother was there, and she asked, "How is Papa?" My grandmother simply said, "He's dead." That was it. No emotion, no nothing.

This was my introduction to death. It made no sense to me. My mother told me that the night after the death, I refused to sleep upstairs. She heard me crying in my sleep asking for my grandfather. I don't remember that. I did think about his odd request of me.

I took that to mean that I should carry on for my grandfather and his legacy. He was involved in starting the union for the garment industry and he stood up for his rights in regard to the workplace. He was the union steward. Grandfather had no sons, so I promised to do good for people and to advocate for the rights of others. I knew I had some "gifts," and I would follow him in his quest to make a difference in people's lives.

After this, if anyone in my family died, I didn't hear about it. After a few months in college, I asked my mom how my aunt Eleanore was. Mom said, "She died." I know she had cancer, but to totally not tell me was strange. My family decided that by keeping the news from me, I wouldn't show emotion or be upset. They thought they were protecting me, but my feelings were hurt because I had no way of having closure with any of my relatives. It was normal to cry and scream and show emotion. Mom would always have a hard time with my crying. She always told me not to cry. But I needed to cry. If I cried, it was a way to release the pain and heartbreak. Then I could begin to heal

How was it in your family? Did people try to hide and deny the death? Did they allow crying? Did anyone in your childhood talk with you about loss and grief? Most people never discuss it. They never got to talk about the deceased loved one for fear it would be overwhelming to those grieving. Most times I meet with people at the time of death, and months later they pretend nothing happened. They block it out somehow. I think we have had a connection. They deny that fact and act like strangers. As long as they know I believe in grief education, they stay clear of me. I wish I were joking, but I am serious. The next story can help me make my point.

My daughter belonged to a sports team. One of the volunteers was a parent of one of the girls on the team. I saw him several times. He looked a little pale, but I didn't think he was sick or anything. He was very well known in our town. I heard one day that this man was exercising and died. He was in his early forties, and he simply died out of the blue. This seemed unreal to me. How can this be? All the parents were terrified that they might be next. A cloud of fear and dread closed in on our community.

There was no formal wake, but his family had everyone come to a local church for a memorial service. Some relatives spoke, but the atmosphere was high anxiety. No one made eye contact, and no one touched one another in the church. I felt very strange because the fear and terror in this church was high. I almost touched another person because we were in the balcony. She shot me an angry look. I am very sensitive and everyone was putting steel over themselves to protect them from the fear they felt. I literally couldn't breathe, and that is not a good feeling.

Afterward they had a reception in the other part of the church. They had tables out for the children to sit and to make signs or cards for the children of the man who died. In that room, I noticed the children naturally going over to the tables, and they started to go around his kids and eat the snacks provided. The support those children received from their peers was touching. My daughter gave her teammate something small to hold. The children laughed and yet they were respectful of the situation.

On the other hand, I never saw one adult eat any of the snacks. They never talked to anyone except their children, and they did so in whispered tones. They went over to the devastated wife, whom I admired for her grace and her heartfelt words. Some people simply left, while the rest of the adults continued to hold their breath and display an odd sense of silence. Here the children were able to give something human to the deceased man's kids. It seemed so loving and so honoring. It looked like honest warmth was between them. It was amazing.

Why were we holding our breath? Why didn't the parents eat the snacks? No adult wanted to "take in" anything of that experience. I know some good friends who helped, but the community was very unnerved by the suddenness of this man's death. I have compassion and empathy for the wife, who was left with young children to raise.

I saw her months later. She was doing the best she could. Her children were involved with sports again, and I prayed for her. She did have siblings and other family to help her. I just wish we could have done more to embrace and comfort her. It seemed as if everyone was so busy protecting themselves, they didn't have any loving energy to give to the family. There was a sense of community, but the children got the best gift of all—love and support.

What do you think about children attending the service? I have no doubt that they were not traumatized by attending. Children under five or six cannot truly understand death. However, if we tell them it is a part of life, maybe we can teach them to deal with death like they deal with life. You can decide for yourself, but remember that not talking about it will not make it go away. My hat is off to those beautiful children who were not afraid to show love and compassion.

I'm so sorry for the untimely death of that man. It taught me that fear doesn't help us cope or deal with reality in an effective way. Showing emotion in our society is a taboo, especially at a funeral. Some brave souls are able to be themselves. The rest of us usually cringe when someone expresses feelings. Most people believe that anyone who laughs at a funeral is being disrespectful. What can we do to lighten up? Can we or should we? Some people laugh when they are nervous.

Chapter 2

Life Purpose and Helping Others

My mission in life is to connect heaven and earth. I have ancient rabbi spirit guides who came to me because of my grief and pain over loss. I would take walks and pour my sorrow out into the universe. I would be crying inside all the time about losing people from my past. These angel rabbis were sick of me crying. They came to me one day and gave me light from the menorah to heal others and myself from the terrible pain of loss.

I knew I had a Jewish soul because my affinity with the Jewish culture and traditions were natural to me. With these guides, I was able to laugh and be happy. I was given a chance to do something wonderful for the world. In Kabbalah, which is Jewish Mysticism, they talk about reincarnation and how we come back to the earth to repair our souls. Therefore, *tikkun* means "to repair." My job is to take people who come to me and help them repair the rips in their soul. This is what I call "spiritual surgery." I will talk about this process later in the book.

Just know that my guides are here to help me grow and to guide my spiritual path toward wholeness and spreading loving kindness to the world. There are three guides. These rabbis are special because they want me to help repair the world. It's not about me, it's about others. Some of the things they ask me to do are very hard. I have learned that if I try to put off what they ask, I will be sorry! Not in a bad way. I still have to do it, so I learned to listen and carry the message to the person they tell me to.

Some of the things they ask me to do are all about helping grieving people. As I stated earlier in the book, I get names, faces, and telephone numbers in my head and I call or pray or both. I get information of a private nature. It's very hard to see the suffering people go through on the healing journey. I can intervene on behalf of my angel guides. They are very loving and have never asked me to do anything but loving gestures. Love is all they send.

There is one piece of the puzzle that is missing in our grief system: that the deceased really are fine, and that their spirit lives on. The hope is that we get to hear from them and feel their presence in our lives. There is an afterlife that is as real as any live person. I have watched many families get signs, gifts, and messages from their lost loved ones. These signs defy logic and yet they happen, especially in cases where the death was sudden and there was trauma to that person. Let's look at the fact that there is life after death, just in a different way than we think. After working with many families who are experiencing grief, I have concluded that the spirit does live on and is aware of what is going on with the family.

I have been to psychic mediums and have heard James Van Praagh and Sylvia Browne talk to the dead. The dead are more interested in what is going on in their loved one's life in the present. Most have an opinion that they want the family to hear. I have witnessed it so many times. I will share these stories in this book, and let you know that you are not alone. Some people don't believe in life-after-death communication. I will be truthful when I say that all the families who experience this are not crazy. Figure it out for yourself after you hear some of the stories.

I understand that fear of the unknown stops people from exploring these concepts, and some refuse to even think about it. We are all human, so some people stay away from funerals and public mourning. No one knows what to do or not do. Just yesterday, the *Chicago Tribune* had an article entitled "Mourning 101" filled with what to do at a funeral. We surely do need more education on what to do when facing a loss. I firmly believe that grief education helps in a way that no other information can.

One of my son's school friend's mom died of a heart virus one day shy of her thirtieth birthday. She had two young children and a husband who loved her. She was very mature for her age, but this was unbearable to our school community. I remember that the daughter, who couldn't be more than four or five, was at the casket with her grandmother.

The grandmother was hysterical and rightly so. The little girl looked at her mom, and the grandmother told her to touch Mommy. The child recoiled and said no. The child was scared of her mom, and she really didn't understand death. She ran from the casket. I wrote this child a letter about how much her mother loved her and about what a great mother she was. They will give this letter to her when she is older.

While at the funeral, the husband's mom had difficulty letting her daughter-in-law go. She was over the casket crying and calling out the deceased's name. I could feel that everyone was very uncomfortable with this outburst of grief. Many people had seen me hug members of the family. Everyone thought that I must be a relative. At least four or five of the people sitting next to me told me to intervene and to make her stop showing her despair and overwhelming grief in such a public way. What she was doing was mourning her daughter-in-law.

Mourning is when you express your feelings over the loss in public. As a clinician, I knew it would be fine to let her grieve. She needed to grieve. She wasn't suicidal or jumping on the casket. It hurt her to lose this woman who was looked upon as a daughter. There were two children left without their mother, who was an amazing woman. The tasks of mourning are to help people adjust to an environment without their lost loved one. For many people, it takes time, space, and patience to fully believe that their lost loved one is really gone.

Another task of mourning is to go forward in life without our lost loved one. I have heard many bereaved parents had money put aside for college, weddings, and other gifts earmarked for the son or daughter they lost. Some still have siblings who remain devastated for years. I have heard from brothers and sisters that they feel as if they had lost their best friend when their sibling died. I often ask parents, "What keeps you going?" Many have other children to raise, so they do have a chance of grandchildren. The hole this makes in the family is huge. That's why when a client asked how she was going to live without her mother, I replied, "One day at a time."

I want to let people know that even though I am a skilled clinician, I will never know the depths of your sorrow, nor do I really know what you actually feel. I won't know the pain unless my child dies, even as an adult. Please know that I am truly sorry for your loss. I can help you through the darkness of the loss and get you into the light again. It will never be the same. This "new normal" is not pleasant, nor is it reversible. Support groups and individual counseling, combined with healthy living, get people through to a life that one of my bereaved parents said would always be "bittersweet."

Back to the family that was dealing with their loss, I wrote the letter to the little girl because I was prompted to write it by God. It was my way to give back to this family the love and acceptance that they gave my children and me. I hope they saved it for the little girl to read when she is old enough to understand about death. I prayed for the family and hope they are not forgetting about their mother, who was a friend of mine.

The sadness of this death was there, and yet there was a basketball game for my son the same day. Can you imagine how awkward that game was for all the parents and children who had recently been to the funeral home? We didn't know what to say, or how to switch the subject to the game. No one talked about the funeral or what it meant to all of us.

We were a school/church family, but we were unable to talk about our feelings. I am sure the boys who played that day felt our uncomfortable feelings and didn't know how to switch to wanting to win the game. We felt lost and powerless; at least I did. No one there was willing to bridge the gap by talking about how difficult the situation was for all of us.

Everyone did help the family out with meals, but we could have done more. How can we make a smoother transition from funerals back to the community without denial? Why are we so afraid to integrate the language of death with the language of life? Right now, death and the aftermath are cut off from our normal day. We can "get over it" quickly and resume life. There is a process that we need to go through before we can heal any loss. This book explains how to move through the stages of grief, not deny or stuff the feelings down that it brings up.

This is often how death is scattered through our days. It often comes without warning, and it is final. Recently, another parent member of our church died in his sleep. He was active in the parish, and was one of the ushers at our service on Sunday. We never spoke except to say hello, but we knew him. When he died, we felt the loss that next Sunday. It was uncomfortable. One day he was here, the next day he wasn't. It is so hard for all of us to realize that life can change in a second.

Often death creeps up on us, and we must honor and respect that people leave in God's time, not ours. It doesn't matter how we are feeling; we must teach our children to understand and accept the funeral rituals and grief process. My daughter, who was eleven at the time, wanted to go to the funeral to support her classmate. We need more compassion and love in this regard. She attends a Catholic school, so it's more accepted to grieve as a school community.

How can we demystify the death process and learn to plan and accept death, not only for others, but also for ourselves? This book can help those who have suffered a recent death, or deal with unresolved grief of someone who died years ago. Unresolved loss is the basis for most of my clients' issues.

If we had more grief information, and took away the taboo of discussing it, the world would be a much happier place. If people knew that life goes on after death, it would comfort them. They could even try to receive messages from their lost loved one on the other side. We also explore these topics in the book. Remember, by talking about death, we can release our fears associated with it and live more fully and in the moment. A trusted therapist years ago put it this way, "We don't have unlimited time [on this earth]."

Let's be earth angels to each other and embrace a friend. Let's share our opinions and help others who are hurting from the loss of a loved one. The more we celebrate life, the more fully we live it. We have this one and only life on this earth. Our soul lessons can be learned through the lens of loss. As we light the darkness, we can reflect the light and the love we felt for our lost loved one and heal ourselves. We can restore ourselves to wholeness, let go of grief, and help others at the same time. It's time to band together and help each other through the darkness. The only way out is through. Let's not think we can do it all alone. Embrace a friend and fly together.

Chapter 3

The God Questions

The first thing people want answered is what happens when people die? Do we go through a door? Is it painful? Do we stop being ourselves? Many near-death experiences have been quoted, and it doesn't seem that traumatic when people report back as they return to the physical body.

The Aramaic word for death translates as "not here" or "present elsewhere." We are asked to think about that. We co-participate in our birth and at our death through the energy mass of our soul. This intelligence, which seems somehow beyond us, is us (p. 138). In other words, we don't realize that life and death are just on a different continuum. There is an order and a divine connection that goes beyond the physical world. Many times we know when we are going to die. This unconscious soul communication leads us to believe that we are born knowing the purpose and plan of our life. We also know when it's time to go. What do you believe?

One man in my grief support group was very special. He was religious, kind, and caring. In November, he gave me an angel calendar and told me, "Thank you for everything." That was odd for him to do. He did make it to the group dinner we had several weeks later. He liked lemon squares, and I got some really good ones to give the group members at dinner. My guides kept telling me not to forget the lemon squares. I didn't know why until a few weeks later, when this man died on his brother's birthday out of the blue. Was it really? Or was it because I had to give him the treat prior to his death. The whole group was shocked when they found out he had passed. Did he somehow know that he wouldn't see me in December?

I have heard many mediums talk to dead people, and they seem to have the same personality in death as they did in life. This makes sense if I think back to my own brother who died. I have been to many mediums, and my brother has never come through. I know my brother was selfless and sensitive to others. My thought is that he lets everyone go before him. He didn't think it was important for him to come through, because other people needed it more. That was his nature.

A friend who was very spiritual told me that in large group meetings, the mediums read the spirits who are assertive, loud, or pesky. Cindi Muntz did a workshop once with me and told me that everyone's relatives were in the room too. She could see them as clear as day. She told me that to figure out if they were dead, she looked down to see if they had feet or not!

In the book *We Live Forever: The Real Truth About Death*, P. M. H. Atwater visits death with the wisdom from the Edgar Cayce Readings. He talks about how it feels to die. He states that, "If you expect to die when you die, you will be disappointed." He writes, "You don't die when you die. You shift your degree of consciousness and change your speed of vibration. That's all death is. A shift" (p. 90).

He tells us that death is like going through a doorway. The only difference is that you are no longer in your body. He states, "The only thing dying does is help you release, slough off, and discard the jacket you once wore. When you die, you lose your body. That's all there is to it. Nothing else is lost."

This is a new concept for most people. The author tells us that death is not as limiting as seems. We change our wavelength like on a radio dial. He says that we are still a spot on the dial, but you move up or down a notch or two. When we change frequencies, we tune in to other "stations." Once you are on a different wavelength, you are no longer compatible with the one you used to occupy on the earth plane.

So can we go beyond and see the spirit world in a different light? That is the question. So ask yourself if you can see in your mind's eye that this other world exists and believe that death does not end life. The biggest gift is that we are still ourselves. Some people have a hard time with that especially if they did not like a certain part of their personality!

I have seen mediums time after time describe the person they are connecting with, and they come through just like they were in life. I had a client who had a reading recently. The medium even captured and demonstrated her father's hand gestures that only she could identify. It made her validate in her mind that indeed, she was seeing her father at that moment. She was able to take in the message he was sending.

What is your view of heaven and hell? I ask this question from anybody I see in therapy. Most people fear God, and are also fearful of Satan. Most people also believe in angels and unseen spiritual help by way of prayer and meditation. Some people in my grief classes try to talk with God, but feel as if they do not get an answer to their prayers. God answers all prayers, at least that's what I believe. He may not answer us in a way that we understand, so we must look for answers ourselves.

The language of the soul and of angels often come from other earth angels in your life. How many times have you needed to hear the words of another person just at the right time? Once people open up a dialogue with God, they can receive an answer. In fact, many times what you ask for might not come to you. When dealing with the higher power (God), you can't always get what you want. Instead of getting mad, think about the fact that you may want something, but that might not be what you need at the time.

There is a saying that if you want to make God laugh, tell him your plans. In twelve-step recovery, we realize that we get what we need. The reality is that by asking, we might not see obstacles or negative consequences that God can see. We want control over the process, but in order to work a successful recovery program, we must surrender our lives and our wills over to the care of God, as we understand him.

It doesn't have to be God but nature, the universe, or whatever represents a higher authority to you. For many years, people have resisted that surrender to God. They let drugs, alcohol, food, sex, or another person rule their lives

As a recovering person, I have said to myself that recovery is overrated. This was part of my disease talking, not my higher self. My higher self is connected directly to my higher power. I must learn to listen to my higher self over my disease, which is not an easy thing to do.

When we work in a spiritual program, we need others around us who are experiencing the same thing. This healing community is set up to make our connection to God and other people closer. People who are addicts believe that there is no higher authority than themselves and/or their drug of choice. We say they are "spiritually bankrupt." We come together in our weakness, and God lifts us to another place where we are free from the compulsion and obsession over these outside things.

The good news is that the twelve-step program helps us fill the emptiness with God, rather than with self-destructive behavior, thoughts, or actions. The beauty of the program lies in the ability to work the spiritual aspect and have spiritual awakenings. These awakenings help us recover and connect us to a helping force of mercy, forgiveness, peace of mind, and self-love.

Opening our heart, we realize that we are worthy of God's love, and we stop being self-destructive. We learn to love and care for ourselves. To work a spiritual program means that we are awake and alive. We can have clarity and a sense of purpose to our lives. We can change our thoughts to match our soul. We can learn to meditate and quiet the mind to let the positive messages in.

Anyone struggling all alone with an addiction can find hope and help with the twelve-step program. It works if you work it. That is the motto that keeps people coming back to meetings and to continue being sober/abstinent. The disease is always waiting to get back in, and that is why relapse is so common. There is no perfect recovery, but part of the program is to "do the next right thing" after a slip-up. One day at a time is designed to avoid anxiety over the future. It's work, and it takes faith, letting go of control and commitment to a new lifestyle.

I know that grieving people are looking for ways to find comfort between the darkness and pain. Darcie D. Sims wrote a book entitled *Why Are the Casseroles Always Tuna?* after the death of her beloved son Austin. He died of a malignant brain tumor in 1976. In her book, she outlines how it took her ten years after his death to allow herself to feel joy again. She states:

> We cannot find words to soothe the hurt. There simply aren't any. We cannot shield ourselves from the twists and turns of living. We can however, build supports and safety nets. We can create cushions and pockets of comfort-places where we can rest momentarily, gathering strength to reenter the crashing tides (p. 12).

She also outlines that grief doesn't have to be a burden and it can be sifted through, reorganized, and dealt with (p. 38). She adds a lighter side of grief that can help us get through the pain. We can choose our next move. I am grateful for her wisdom, as she knows firsthand how losing a child can affect the family. Allow yourself some fun, and know that your lost loved one would rather see a smile on your face than a frown. Open your heart to the light, and drink in the white light from the heavens. The light will help you begin to experience joy again.

Connecting with the power of Kabbalah is another way to recover from addiction and help people spiritually. Kabbalah means "to receive." It is not a religion or cult but technology for the soul. These tools for transformation contain universal principles and are over two thousand years old. Kabbalah is based on an ancient manuscript of the Zohar written by Shimon Bar Yochai. He explains that the true meaning behind the stories of the Bible are written in code. This code contains the knowledge of how the universe functions.

Light is the energy of sharing; fulfillment and goodness are infinite. We need to look for security and contentment in the 99 percent realm. This is the realm that is spiritual and goes beyond the five senses. In other words, it is invisible. The light resides inside physical things. It's not the money we want, it's the light that resides in the money. We have an opponent built into the creation process by design. This opponent is called Satan—code word for chaos.

There are two broadcasts in the universe. We have free will to choose which one we will manifest. The reactive broadcast is an illusion and contains the 1 percent world. This 1 percent world is limited to our physical world and includes only what we can see, hear, taste, smell, and feel. The reactive thought tells us that it's the other person who has the problem. This contains the ego. The reactive voice tells us that we can receive for the self alone. We project blame on other people.

The proactive thoughts remind you that it's not about the other person. It's about you and your reactive nature that is the problem. When you receive the proactive energy, it also fills up the physical lacks that exist. We can therefore receive for the sake of sharing. Satan's greatest trick is to make you believe that he is invisible. Satan is a trickster. This creates fragmentation. Where is the Satan in your life?

Kabbalah wisdom suggests that the physical world is an illusion (1 percent). The five senses are a block to spirituality. We can get in touch with the energy of the soul by having a healthy thought. Once we become conscious of this system, we can begin to tune in to the proactive thoughts. These proactive thoughts help us to plug into the 99 percent spiritual world. When we embark on a soul journey, we can be proactive or reactive. Consciousness opens the cosmic door. This ancient energy of the soul regenerates our ability to balance our world for peaceful means.

Remember, Kabbalah is a system. It's a different way of thinking about the world. All is connected. It's about sharing, listening, and being proactive. The reactive system of thinking does not bring anything especially the light. Being reactive and thinking reactive thoughts lead to chaos and darkness. People start thinking about their ego and not about sharing with other people.

This is darkness, and Satan and evil exist in a chaotic world. In fact, darkness is built into the very design of creation. This increases our distance from God. The path to God through evil is forbidden. God continues to be unchanged by what we do. We cannot change our nature or achieve transformation if we cleave to a life devoid of sharing, compassion, and kindness.

Everything that exists does so because God created it, and because God's creative flow continues to sustain us. We have free will, so we can make our choice. We can live in the light or bring light to dark places. Spiritual receivers give us the ability to tap into the light, love, and proximity to God. We cannot merge with God, as some distance must remain.

The light is always on. We can't see it because there are blankets covering our spiritual vision. We can call them veils, as they cover our soul lights. The goal is to awaken this energy that is around our soul to increase love and light and to open our hearts to God's will for us. How do we know about the 99 percent world of the endless? If you don't know about it, you cannot tap into it! There needs to be a constant supply of gratitude and appreciation of this light. We can connect to fulfillment, eliminate chaos, and maintain that connection to fulfillment if we can learn to be proactive.

We can connect to secret energy and hidden light that emanates from our soul. It is said that Mozart tapped into the 99 percent. These principles are universal in nature and predate religion. We can unblock hidden fear, anger, jealousy, and judgment by connecting to the light. The spiritual light can control our ego and bring more meaning and purpose to our life.

The best part about Kabbalah is that it is being shared with the entire world. It was never meant for specific people. In ancient days, only men who were scholars over forty or fifty were allowed to learn Kabbalah. We need fragmentation to stop in this world. We can help the world by sharing and believing in something we can't see.

Chapter 4

The Process of Letting Go

What exactly is letting go? Does it mean to "get over it" and move on? What do we do when letting go means that we give up control of thoughts in our mind? Buddhists are very good at focusing on the present moment. We call this "mindfulness" in therapy terms. The skill of mindfulness is to focus on the here and now.

I like to use the song "Let It Be" by The Beatles. I also bring in Mother Mary when the song goes, "When I find myself in times of trouble, Mother Mary comes to me, speaking words of wisdom, 'let it be.'" I didn't realize that the name of Paul McCartney's mother was really Mary. This is very calming to me.

If I put it in divine hands, then I must trust what the answer is. What can we do when a loved one is gone? We are powerless over God's choices in this regard. If the person was murdered or in the case of suicide, we have special circumstances. However, it doesn't matter how someone passes; we are many times still dazed, shocked, and confused about what happened.

Grieving people look for "signs" that their loved ones are around. It could be a special song. It could be found pennies. It could be a number that keeps showing up. If people look for these signs, they are not crazy. They are receiving confirmation that their lost loved one is okay. Sometimes they come in our dreams, or a person says something that he used to say.

If it helps the grieving person, then let it be real. Sometimes people have license plates with their name on it in front of you on the roadway.

This is God's way of sending you hope and cheer. Some people like to go to a psychic medium for answers. I can't say that they are the answer to everything, but they are a piece in the grief recovery process. Not everyone goes this route. That's okay, there is no wrong or right way to grieve. If you don't believe in "signs," that's okay too.

Those of us who think they are bargaining with God are furious when they can't stop a loved one from dying. They can't do anything to make the other people change. People have free will. If you want to destroy yourself, you can do it. You can do it fast, or you can do it slow.

Losing someone in an accident, you realize they had no control. Many times the people involved in the accident didn't know they were going to die. They lost control and we are upset because we weren't with them. The last thing a mom or dad thinks about is whether they were in pain. Did they suffer? Those who have loved ones who died in another state, country, or continent wish they could have been there and/or they could have said goodbye.

I once witnessed a car accident one sunny day in July over ten years ago. I was on my way to an exercise studio. I went a different way that day and my gut told me to deliberately go a different way. It was a very conscious thought. I parked my car and heard a deafening silence. I looked in the direction of the quiet and saw people get in their cars and leave. I walked to the corner and noticed that a young girl had been run over by a dump truck.

It was horrible to see. She was twelve and was going to the high school on her bike. She was there and I started praying. I met another women at the scene who told me she had seen the girl go under the truck, and how traumatized she was by seeing that. If I had gone my normal route, my car would have been in the same spot as the woman's was. I would have seen what the other lady had seen and felt.

I don't think I could live with that picture in my mind. I felt I should stay with her on the street and just pray. I wondered how her mother would have felt, thinking her daughter was alone. The truck driver did not see her in the crosswalk because he was up too high in the truck. He was making a right-hand turn and didn't realize he had hit a young girl. He was stunned.

I was able to write the mother a letter, and told her that caring people had been there, and that we were all crying for the girl. I won't go into detail, but there was no doubt that she passed away before the ambulance came. I asked at the hospital and the nurse couldn't believe that I didn't know she passed quickly.

I got back an angel card from the girl's mother. The angel looked just like her daughter. I sent over an angel to her house, and she had a beautiful water-bearer statue put into the garden in front of the gas station where her daughter passed away. Over the years I have seen many balloons, little stuffed animals, candles, and flowers placed there to remember the girl's birthdays and her loss. I know she was so loved. Every time I pass the memorial, I say hello. I will never forget the day she passed. My heart goes out to her parents and brother. She will forever be missed and loved. I am so glad that I reached out to her mother.

People always ask me why. "Why did God take my son or my daughter? What did I do to get this?" As we know, bad things happen to good people all the time. I don't know why anything happens. The stories of loss that I have heard are very difficult to comprehend. These people were smart, charming, and beautiful. Their lives were bursting with options and they had a great support system. They were like lights in the family—bright and happy and so alive.

I want to let you know that the reincarnation explanation is that when we were in heaven, we made a chart. This chart told about what family we would be born to. The chart outlined what we wanted to work on in this lifetime and included when we are born and when we die. Some people die earlier than later. Remember, we forget all this once our soul is in the body and we are born.

Some of these souls enter and exit as a miscarriage. I even had one of those. It was hard to understand. Some have physical and mental disabilities. My own twin brothers never grew up and had a normal life. Their mental illnesses stopped them from attending college, having a successful career, and having loving wives and children.

As I have stated, one of my brothers died in a hit-and-run accident in California at age forty. My other brother is alive and, at fifty-four, lives in a group home in New York. He smokes and lives a marginal life, not what I would have picked for him.

I am still not sure I believe the reincarnation theory. Having been born Catholic and then studied Kabbalah (Jewish Mysticism), I am still confused. I still pray every week in church, light candles, and pray for multiple people daily. My prayers are constant throughout the day.

Still, it is very hard to live with the knowledge that one's child, spouse, friend, or other loved ones die, and we may never know why. Just know that it was not to punish you. God does not take people for revenge. We are born with free will. We simply can't control when we are born and when we die. This is the human condition, and it makes us powerless and vulnerable.

I have begged God to help my dad live when all he wanted to do was die. I asked for mercy for him. I saw how hard it was for him not to be able to walk or take a simple shower by himself. He couldn't take being trapped at an assisted-living home. He made the decision about the DNR order. God took him and now he is home in heaven.

What my clients' families have going for them is that they did some things that gave them hope and meaning to their sons' and daughters' lives. They developed scholarships and planted trees in dedication to the child who died. They formed foundations and groups that would understand the pain they were experiencing. They honored the memory of that child, whether he be four, sixteen, or twenty-two. They go to the cemetery and have rituals during anniversary dates.

One client was very close to her dad. On the anniversary of his death, she did everything he would have done in a day. She went to all the same restaurants, all the same errands, and ate his favorite food—ribs. She even buried one by his grave so he could have one too! We need these rituals to heal. This was her way to connect with her dad and show her love for him.

I was recently speaking to a group of funeral directors about spirituality, and most of the people did not put their own wellbeing above that of the clients. It was clear that self-care was not number one on the list for them. Especially when working in a business where death is the norm, it is hard not to get depressed or be full of darkness. I am so impressed with the love and care they give others. If they gave more to themselves, it would be easier to navigate the loss and grief of others.

The funeral home I work with deals with deaths of all kinds. Since there is no organized time to die, they are hit with many different families all at the same time. They handle suicides, homicides, children, the very old, babies, and all kinds of deaths. It takes a special kind of person to work there.

I admire all my colleagues at Adolf Funeral Home, both the Berwyn and the Willowbrook, Illinois, locations. They are amazing, they go above and beyond for people, and have talented and compassionate staff who truly want to help. They offer counseling and a monthly grief group, free of charge, to take care of the grieving families. If you ever need a funeral home, go to an Adolf Funeral Home. They are family owned and operated. I am honored to work with them to help grieving families.

How do we rise out of the darkness and embrace the light of our soul? The first step is to desire light. The second is to have a relationship with the divine and to ask for guidance and signs. The third is to believe that the power of God can restore us to wholeness. We need to surrender to God because we are not above him. Many people think surrender means death, or that they are weak.

The real answer is that it's just the opposite. Only healthy people know that if they continue to do what they have always done, they will always get what they always got. You have to change the way you think and the way you see the world before you can begin to get out of the darkness. You have to see how dangerous the dark is for your spirit and soul.

There are ways people can let go of their grief and still honor and remember their lost loved one. I was thinking about doing a grief group at our church/school. One priest wanted to start a bereavement group. One widowed lady had just lost her husband, and she got no acknowledgment from the church. No one called her and offered comfort after her husband died. She was business minded, smart, and a very capable woman. She started the Compassionate Care Ministry along with Father Watkins at St. Cletus Church in LaGrange, Illinois.

I knew that my getting this position was no accident. This is how God works. In my case, I fit right in because I have had many losses in my life. My goal was to let go of the past, use the spirituality that I know helps, and teach people what I need to learn. We teach what we most need to learn.

There is a quote that comes from a poem that says, "With every goodbye, you learn." Let's open up our hearts and souls to healing the hurts of yesterday, so we can enjoy the joy of today! You can't feel the joy if you can't feel the pain. Let us begin with hope that life can begin again after a devastating loss.

Chapter 5

The Process of Forgiveness, Not Forgetting

Two years ago today, I was at my father's hospital bed in New York with deep sorrow knowing they were going to take him off the ventilator. I was crying and hoping he could hear me. I was awakened at 5:30 a.m. that day by a doctor at Huntington Hospital. He told me that something happened to my dad the night before, and that they had put him on a ventilator.

He was staying in an assisted-living residence, and continued to suffer from an ailment that had been his companion for almost two years. He had an intestinal problem that made him upset. He couldn't control his bowels. He couldn't walk by himself, and he hated being in the assisted-living facility. He complained that no one talked to him, as they were more impaired than he was.

He wanted to die so badly that every night when I called him, he would say "DNR, Karen." I knew he wanted to die because when I said to him, "You're not going anywhere," he put his head down and sighed. He was tired of fighting the illness, which caused him to wear diapers and have diarrhea daily.

Dad was depressed, but he wanted to go home to God. Knowing this, he had to get off the ventilator. Somehow the doctors didn't realize he had a DNR in place. They told me they would take out the machine when I got there. It took me twelve hours to get there. I just lost it. I was

crying and knew that this time he would get his wish to die. At least I
could help him carry out one of his final wishes.

It appeared that he couldn't hear me sob. I was there for over three
hours until a technician pulled the tube out that was forcing air down
his throat. They made me leave the room as they took out the tubing. I
heard my dad try to say something, so I knew he could talk.

As soon as I was back in the room, my dad asks, "Am I dying?" He
doesn't acknowledge that I was there crying my eyes out. I don't know
what he was seeing, because that is an odd question. At first I said no.
Then my denial broke and I realize that I have to tell him he is dying.
I start talking, telling him it will be fine, and now that the machine is
gone, he can leave and go home to heaven. I don't know how long I was
talking, but I tend to babble when I am scared.

Dad listened for a few minutes, and then he moved his head closer
to me and struggles to say, "Will you stop talking? You are waking me
up!" I was floored. The last thing my dad says to me is to stop talking?
I did feel bad, but I stopped talking. Something was going on with
him, and he didn't want to be disturbed. No goodbye, no thanks, just
be quiet. I obeyed his wish.

By 11:00 p.m., nothing happened to his heart rate or his breathing.
My guides told me I could go, and that I didn't have to sit with him
until the last breath. I am grateful. The nurse on duty told me that it
could take a long time, or it could be quick. It wasn't something that
can be rushed. I decided to go to the hotel. The nurse told me that they
close the front door after midnight, and how to get back to the ICU in
case it was three or four in the morning.

As I sat there in the silence, I prayed for mercy for my dad. With
all the abuse he did to me, he suffered. He never admitted anything to
me, but I did tell him that I forgave him. He said, "For everything?" I
said, "For everything."

Even on his deathbed, I am crying because I know that by being
there, I was repairing the split inside myself. I was asking for mercy for
a man who hurt me far worse than anyone in my life. It was me who
had to ask for mercy for him, nobody else could do it.

I cried when I thought about all the hateful letters I sent him over
the years, all the anger I showed him, and how I turned my back on him
and hardened my heart. I remembered how I turned the rage on myself;

hating myself with a passion; wanting to abuse, punish, kill, and starve myself. All that self-loathing, depression, and pain, I put on myself.

It finally came to the truth. I no longer needed to punish myself or him for dirty deeds he committed. I too could fly away from that dark and evil place inside myself. I could let go of the past, and create love where there was hurt and light where there was darkness. I could break the family spell of abuse. I could be cleansed, I could be loving toward both him and myself. I cried silently to myself, and I saw what I did to myself because I was abused. I could leave it in the past, and the self-hate and evil could also be released from my soul. I could finally give God my soul to cleanse.

Asking for mercy for him healed me. God told me that by asking for mercy for him, I was now free of the chains that made me a victim all these years. I told my story to a client who also suffers from childhood wounds, and she actually asked if I ever thought I would ask God for mercy for him. I replied that I never thought I would ever have enough compassion for him and his suffering. I surprised myself.

My dad was punished for his sins, and he paid for them. He lost his forty-year-old son, the son he was closest to. My dad told me he had a dream a year before my brother Michael was killed in a hit-and-run in California. In the dream, he was told that my brother would die. Dad never spoke of the dream until after Michael passed. He was hit by a full-sized van. It was heartless, and the man got away. Dad had the death certificate hidden away. My brother was his light, his pal, and his hope. He knew he was sick, and hated that he couldn't get married and have his own kids. It was both sad and tragic. Both his sons never grew up.

My brother James is more mentally ill than Michael. He lives in a group home because he cannot work or function on his own. He always needs to be taken care of. He rarely talks, unless he is asking for something. He remembers some of the past, but suffers from dementia at age fifty-four.

During the time I was silent in the room, there was a TV that had soothing sounds and scenes from nature. I kept looked at the mountain scenes on the screen and heard birds chirping. It was soothing as well as majestic. I couldn't stand the birds, but my guides told me that that is where he was going. He was going to a majestic place with nature and birds, almost like a paradise.

I finally understood why he wanted me to be quiet. That is where he was going. I was glad that I was able to give him the freedom to fly home. My dad's neighbor told me later that Dad used to feed the birds early each morning. His neighbor says he can still see my dad out there each morning feeding the birds. I chose a prayer card of a soaring eagle flying through the air. The words "Going Home" gave me a good feeling. He was going to his home, to see his relatives. I hope Michael was there to meet him as he crossed over.

The hospital called me at 3:30 a.m. to say his heart rate was low. I flew there, but it was too late. He was gone by 3:45 a.m. I knew he wanted it that way. They had left him as he was, with his mouth wide open and eyes shut. It seemed as if he might have been gasping for air, and it bothered me to see him so lifeless. I didn't linger at the bedside. I knew he was gone and happy to be free of his body. He couldn't control the things he used to, and for him, there was peace in the silence. He was home at last. He didn't have to suffer anymore; he could be united in heaven with those he loved, and be loved back.

I could go on and live a happier life. I felt free from confusion and fear. I could give up the ghost of childhood past. Dad and the abuse no longer lingered in my brain. It was almost like in the Wizard of Oz. The wicked witch is dead! Dad had left this world, and I completed the past with love instead of hate.

I saw him as a person who was also a victim of abuse by his father, not some kind of monster that stalked my consciousness. I no longer heard his voice telling me that I ruined myself, or that I was "a sick girl." I trusted that God would bring me out of my victimhood. I was more than a survivor. I repaired the trauma and the deep rip that was in my heart. I felt whole for once in my life.

Making Peace with the House My Grandfather Built

There was still more work to be done after the funeral. We had to sell Dad's house. When I went to visit Dad in the assisted-living place, he was angry at me. He said that I was there because I wanted his house and his money. I was floored. The thought of me living in his house made me physically ill. I had no idea how much money he really did have. He had added me as the beneficiary on some but not on others.

When he said that I wanted his money and house, he couldn't be more wrong. I knew I would be left to clean it out and get it ready for sale. Just the thought of doing this for him made my skin crawl. Who knew how much mold was on the walls. The place seemed dirty and neglected. Some of the walls were black because he never painted them.

The only difference was that Dad had put in a tub and expanded the bathroom. They still had a makeshift shower in the basement. The bottom of it was concrete, and I hated using that shower. It had a curtain, no door. It was cold and damp down in that basement. The thought of having to clean it was too much for my psyche to handle.

Dad was very upset in the assisted-living home. He told all the people he was glad to be there. In reality, he was not happy. He couldn't breathe when they went downstairs for any group meeting. No one would talk to him in the dining hall, and there wasn't much to do there.

When I asked him if he wanted to transfer to another home, he declined. He kept going back to the hospital, because they only had a doctor at the home once or twice a week. He couldn't walk well, and he told me he couldn't take it. He wanted to go home to heaven.

His neighbor knew if he went home to his house, he would fall again. I was stuck in the middle. He couldn't go home because it was filled to the brim, and there was only room for him to lie down. If someone came to the house to help him, it would have been tight quarters. Also, the neighbor knew he would be asked to intervene if something happened. I couldn't do that to his neighbors. He has no safety features like lifeline to help him.

It was hard to see him in the assisted living, but it didn't make sense to send him home when everyone in the neighborhood was scared he would die in the house or call them to help since he was alone. During the months prior to his original fall, he was anxious and upset. He would knock on neighbors' doors at midnight or later, or he would fall and ask them to come over.

One of his neighbors, Ted, was wonderful to him. Ted told me that the last time Dad fell, he was crying because he couldn't walk. Ted also told me Dad had no will to live, and might self-abuse. John was another neighbor who helped Dad out. Both of these men and their wives acted like relatives and helped him. I have never seen anything like it before. There were angels who helped him and people who gave him food, clothes, warmth, and hope. These neighbors were his family of choice. He had more friends than I did.

Another angel was Jim, who lived down the block. He wanted the house and was willing to pay $190,000 for it as is. He would help me clean the house and take out the furniture, and told me not to kill myself trying to clean it. However, I had to make peace with that house. It was just something I had to do alone.

My friend from college, Michele, was angry with me regarding the house. She wanted to come and help me. I didn't know it until I was done. She said she could have done a mitzvah for me. Who knew that? My cousin Lenore also asked if she could help. I felt I had to prove to myself that I could handle that house and all that was in it.

Dad had an obsession with the dark side, so there were items that reflected this. He had religious statues there as well. It was so creepy with both light and dark parts. There was a religious part of Dad, but when my brother was killed, Dad turned to the darkness. He did turn the statues to the front again but never felt like they were helping him.

Dad told me that he couldn't make sense of my brother's death. He wasn't shot in a war, so Dad couldn't say he died for his country. He died because some person in a big van ran him over in what seemed to be either bad timing or a random act. Dad had hid the death certificate and had never recovered.

On the table in the dining room was a new box of sneakers. Dad had wanted to send them to him. Now they were useless. When I cleaned out all the closets, I put them into a box that collected clothes and shoes for the poor. I know my brother would have wanted it that way.

I approached the house as a challenge. My job was to throw out all the negative energy and evil influences in the house. I prayed for cleansing. I knew I had the power to make the job into a healing project. I always felt the house was creepy, with all the hidden family secrets and bad karma. I had to cleanse this house and myself of Dad's sins and obsessions. I had to feel the fear of being there alone. I used the power of God to help me. My spirit guides were there trying to make me laugh at the craziness of the situation. This was between my dad and myself.

Inside the house, I saw a picture of Dad on a horse. I was wondering when that was. Dad told me to give it to a family he knew from the flea market. His name was Jeff. I gave him anything he wanted from the garage. When I gave him the picture, I said that my dad wanted him to have it, but I didn't know why. Jeff said that Dad got on the horse when he attended one of his kids' birthday parties. I was very surprised. Dad was smiling in the picture, like he was having fun. I knew nothing about his connections. He always acted so lonely, but he wasn't!

Dad was always suspicious of my motives. For years, whenever he went to the hospital, he would not tell me. He would give his neighbor Ted the keys to his house and his wallet. He would tell Ted, "Don't let anyone in my family inside my house." Do you know it was years before my Dad ever told me he used to go to the hospital frequently? He told me he was cured of prostate cancer. I was shocked. He never told me anything.

My mom knew, but she lived in another town. It was years before my dad gave me the keys to his house. He let Ted get his mail but not me. I knew nothing about where his money was, or how much he had. He lived like a hermit. He slept on the same cot for over fifty years. He rarely cleaned, and his walls were blackened from the dirt. Dad ate very cheaply too.

He had many bowel obstructions due to complications of being shot in the stomach during the Korean War. Dad was a leader in the war, a sergeant. He never talked about his disability. As a disabled veteran, he collected money. However, when he wanted to go to a Veterans Administration housing facility, they told him he wasn't disabled enough. Dad was heartbroken. He was so angry. I don't blame him. It was sad. He did have a purple heart that was awarded to him in his later years. He was very proud of this honor.

When I was finally able to put all the pieces together about my dad, he was very different from the father I knew as a child. When he was young and married to my mother, it was always chaotic. He would be frustrated and angry most of the time. He had a very bad temper. He was strong and his violent ways were how he ran the house.

Mom was abused as well. He was angry with my mom for being sick. He was angry because my brothers had special needs. I understand he was an only child who was neglected and spent much too much time alone. He wasn't treated well and married a woman who had a mental illness. They divorced because of his violent and abusive ways. He moved in with my grandparents around the block from us.

I don't envy my dad's life, but in the later years, he began to calm down and was still there for my brothers whenever they needed him.

Both my parents were sad that my husband wasn't interested in creating more of a connection with them as in-laws. That was their only chance for a healthy son. I was wrong not to help my husband do this. It is something I haven't forgiven myself for yet. My mom cried as my dad told her, "He is not going to call us Mom and Dad." I wish this were different. I just have to turn this over to God. I wished I had told my parents that I was sorry.

Having regrets and not forgiving ourselves are the worst things we can do. They tie us to the past and continue to shame and traumatize us as we grow older. Many people haven't forgiven themselves yet just like me. Of course, my mom and dad needed to divorce. That split affected me much more than I was willing to admit.

The loss of my dad was never talked about. I never admitted missing him. I never admitted I was furious at him either. I wasn't allowed to have my feelings. I had to sneak food and cry in the dark just to soothe myself. I was like countless other little girls and boys who were made into instant parents to their siblings without ever knowing how to be a parent. We were children operating in a mixed up family system, no one to tell me to do my homework or to care where I was.

Mom was just surviving too. What choice did she really have? She was powerless over her illness and her smoking habit. She fought for my brothers and me so we could have a good life. She fell and got up again, over and over. Her will was very strong. She would get sick, and it was me who tried to hide her illness from my dad and from the world. I was co-dependent with both of them. Why did I have identity issues? Who was I? Where did I begin? How can I get out of my house and get away from the craziness? There were many times I had no answers to my questions. I was lonely and empty on most days.

I had to pretend all was well. I got to be good at it. If you had similar feelings about your childhood, know that I understand all the fear and shame. For me, with the grace of God and a few good friends and neighbors, I was told that I could to go to college. Let me tell you, it was a long road, and there were relationship issues from being in that environment that I brought to college with me.

I know I had an angry side of me and that I abused myself with negative thinking. I believed that I wasn't good enough and inferior to others. This continued to play out for me in many ways. Now I was in his house, and had more work to do. Perhaps I could heal the pain from my childhood by facing my fear of being alone in the house.

I called in my spirit guides. I verbally called out any evil entity that might be there in the darkness. I threw out all voodoo and evil pictures, and denounced Satan and all the mental illness, paranoia, and bad energy that was in the house. I spent a lot of time going through pockets of old clothes. Dad did pull a few jokes on me. Prior to his dying, he told me that there was money hidden everywhere. He said money was in clothes pockets, under the rug, under the fan, in boxes, and told me I would have to go through everything to find it. I told him that was crazy, and that he should take it all out before he died. No such luck there.

There I am, spending one day in the basement alone, looking in countless pockets, trying to pick up old rugs, and going through everything so I would find the money. After almost a day finding nothing, I asked my dad aloud where the money was hidden. I said, "Dad, if there is money here, show me where it is!" I was furious and being down there was scary, even in the daytime. All I heard back from him was, "Made you look!" This was not funny to me at all.

I also found out that my dad was an organized person. He told me where the lock box was with all his important papers. The only problem was that he didn't show me where the key was to open the box. He told me where it might be. He told me I would have to look for it. Great, I thought, another game I must play. I took every key in the house, and nothing fit. I could hardly move the box since it was one of those big, steel-like boxes with a lock on the front. I dragged it down the stairs—it was heavy. When I got it to the kitchen, I tried every key I had. I knew I might have to break the lock. So getting tired of playing the game, I took a hammer and banged it until it opened.

Just then, my dad's neighbor came to the door. He knew how secretive my dad was with his personal items. Just as I opened the box, the phone rang once. The phone never rang before, and this was the first time.

Ted picked it up, and I said, "Who is it?"

He looked at me and said "dead."

I said, "Oh no, it was my dad. He is telling us that he knows I am in his stuff!"

Ted said, "Are you feeling all right?"

I said yes to him. My dad was there, and later I found the key in an apron he had covering the back of his easy chair in the living room. What good was it doing there?

All the papers were in order, covered in plastic, and stapled together.

I did find something near my dad's bed that immediately took away my anger and replaced it with compassion. In the house he had cards that my brother Michael had sent him from California. They were all written to my dad, whom my brother called "Daddy Warbucks." They were all positive letters, thanking my dad for his help and for bringing him light and laughter. I realized that my brother's death stopped my dad's light from coming in. He had my brother's ID from the accident, all torn and dirty next to his bed. His pouch that he wore was there too. Dad had hidden his death certificate under some papers and forgot about it.

My other brother James, who is Michael's twin, never was well enough to send cards, or to laugh with my dad. James was more of a child and needed to be taken care of. Michael was his grown son. He was mentally ill, but he was kind and loving to my dad. When my brother died, my dad was crying when they tried to close the casket. My brother died in a tragic way, and it was violent and gruesome. Dad never forgave himself for not being there. He did send away for the pictures of the accident site. They were gruesome too, and this only added to his sorrow.

So the house was a mixed bag. On one hand, we have a person who is very organized, very structured, and very modest. On the other hand, we have confusion between being Catholic and dabbling in the occult. We have dark, negative energy that is a sign that there was mental illness. We have a man who didn't think to spend any money on upgrades, cleaning, and taking care of the inside of a house.

Outside, it looks like a cute house. On the inside I found out that two of the three children never grew up. The tragedy that was my family was very obvious. I found sorrow, pain, and depression. The only pictures of my brothers were when they were in highchairs. They looked so cute, but there was brain damage and more illness on the way.

The only picture of me older was my college graduation photo. I looked away from the camera. One could see that I was pretty, but I couldn't face myself. In that picture I saw someone confused about the world. It was hard to look myself in the face. No one in my family had ever gone to college or earned a degree. No one understood why I wanted to go to graduate school. It was a struggle for me too. How could I live a happy life with all the mental illness, pain, sorrow, and depression that enveloped me? I guess for the first time, I had compassion for myself.

I was no longer angry with my father and mother. They were dealt bad cards. They were both only children together with no skills and no communication ability. It was a godsend they divorced. Together, they had no chance for a happy marriage. I was sad that I had to take over being the parent when I was very young. I forgave myself for all the "bad" parenting that I gave to my brothers. I had no idea what I was doing.

It was good this house was there for my dad. He had a reading with Sylvia Browne, who actually told him that the house was "dead" and for him to move out. He could never move out. This was his life: anorexic and rigid. Dad never spent money on himself, never was able to break out from just surviving, never gave himself anything. He lived like a miser. He thought that was "good enough for him."

His only pleasure was the flea market. There, he came alive and had a full life for one day a week. Now that the house is gone, he was right—it was his therapy. I left that house knowing that the man who was buying it would clear out all of the furniture and old memories.

I knew he wasn't going to bulldoze over the house. He was going to take it and add onto it. He would knock down walls, add a room upstairs, and freshen the place up. Dad's legacy would go on. The buyer Jim would continue on in the house. There was no longer any trace of tragedy. All the time they lived in the house, they did the best they could. I felt confident that I had made peace with both the house and with my family. I would have to live on for them—especially my brother Michael.

Dad's neighbors, Ted and Betty, told me that the lesson for me is that I don't have to live the life my father did. I don't have to live in a rigid, anorexic way. I can spend money on vacations, food, and not live in so much fear. I can enjoy my kids, and hopefully, they can grow up in a healthy way. I could choose not to be victim for what my dad had done to me. I was a survivor, and so were my parents. I don't have to grieve so hard. I know that they are happy on the other side. My dad got his wish—he got to go home to God. My mother is no longer sick in heaven. She doesn't need to smoke every minute of the day. She is whole and at peace.

Mom and Michael are together in one grave. My dad is buried up high in a mausoleum. My brother James will join him when it is time. I have no idea where I will be for eternity yet. I will tell you this: I no longer want to leave the planet anymore. I have dug myself out of the past, and I leave it be. I focus on what I have, and by going and facing my dad's house and his life, I am not afraid to live. I wish that things had resolved sooner, but now that it's done, I know I did the right thing by forgiving my dad and mom. It's just James and me left. Since he lives in a group home in New York, I visit him as much as I can. I can truly be his sister now. I get to tell him to get a haircut, take a shower, and trim his beard. He is such a child, but I accept him as he is.

Chapter 6

Light versus Dark

Our guardian angels are there for us, but they cannot intervene without us asking for help. Most people don't believe that they have angels or angelic guidance, but I have always believed. I must have asked a million times for help, and each time, I have received help. It may have come to me in a thought or in songs I hear in my head. It might come from another person saying something to me, or I hear it in a homily at church. No matter what, if you learn the language of the soul, you can decode any message.

To read the messages of the soul, you first need to believe that we have a soul. We then need to believe in the big picture. We have an inner consciousness that is divine and soul based. We are interconnected to everything here on earth. Earth is the school and heaven is where the spirits are. Our soul leaves the physical body after death. In Kabbalah, there are different parts of the soul that leave the body after death. Some parts stay with the body for a length of time. In religious terms, the soul goes up at death and that's it. I have had a relative tell me that when her mom was dying, she actually witnessed the soul leaving the body. I haven't heard that very often.

Tikkun is a very special word from Kabbalah and it means "to repair." According to the great teachers of Kabbalah, the world was formed by the big boom theory. They explain it as in the beginning, all there was was the light and a vessel to receive light. The endless light gave to the vessel, but the vessel couldn't give back light. After a while, the vessel felt shame for receiving light and not being able to do anything in return or give anything to earn the light.

The example explained to me was that how many times would you go to lunch with somebody and let them pay before you would get frustrated. After a while, we would all stop going to lunch with this person. That's exactly what happened in the endless world. You would have to eat "bread of shame," or eating without having to do anything for it. Not earning it, just eating for free. The vessel finally said "stop" to the light and then the vessel blew up in a thousand pieces; hence, the big bang.

Pieces went everywhere and became fragments. The ancient Kabbalist scholars say that in life, we are to find these "holy sparks" and raise them to wholeness. Each time we become like the light, we are repairing the world. This is how each one of us learn our lessons and do our part in repairing the world.

The rabbis always show me a big planet with me sewing up the holes and the ripped parts. They tell me that it helps every time we show love and offer light to others. Being a beacon of light also heals our heart and soul, and helps us to be effective and energized. The image of sewing the world up includes making very precise stitches and making sure that what I am sewing up is done with utmost care.

A friend of mine had surgery for boils that grow all over her torso. The surgeon did a great job on the initial repair, but after a while, the repairs were not like the first ones. I could tell that the doctor had gotten tired of being so focused and precise. This is why the rabbis only let me do small pieces at a time. They don't tell me why I am asked to help in this regard. If they tell me to do anything, I do it. They never give me a project that is overwhelming to the extent that I cannot perform up to their standards.

My rabbi guides are right not to tell me the big picture while I am working on a piece. They send people to me and then only reveal what I need to know. When the "project" is completed, I am told to either walk away or complete a final piece. I met one such lady at a funeral home lecture I was giving about life after death several years ago. At the time, she was wearing a hat because she was bald from chemotherapy. She came in late but was very much of a presence. I had seen her before in another workshop I did at the church several months back. I didn't know her name, but she was telling me that her life was similar to a popular male psychic medium we both knew.

The lady named Joan had spoken out about how great it was to talk about life after death at a church meeting. Father Watkins and I, along with the bereavement ministry we started, did the workshop together. A lot of elderly people came, and they were very interested about what heaven was like. We spoke about what they thought it was like in heaven and hell. We also talked about purgatory and if that place really existed. We talked about signs or messages that our loved one sent us from heaven. It was amazing that people had signs and messages but never really thought about it. They sometimes said these things were coincidences, weird, crazy, or random.

Joan knew the truth. She had been involved in psychic discussions, and had a brilliant mind. I knew right away this lady had some experiences that we all could hear, confirming that life goes on after death. When she came in, the rabbis said, "Let her talk." I stepped away from the podium and asked her to tell us her experiences. Some of the stories were amazing! She was a good speaker, and very good at telling these stories. I was impressed. After the workshop, I heard, "Watch over her." I knew I had to listen and to help her.

When God told me to watch over her, I took that to mean that I was involved in helping her on the journey to health. It didn't feel at all overwhelming. I didn't know if she would die or not, just that I should befriend her. I did what I was told. I was instructed to bring her angels and other gifts of the spiritual nature. She believed that she had untapped potential in the psychic arena, but didn't know how to go to the next level.

She gave a few readings to people and went on expeditions to experience the spirit with a trusted male friend. He later admitted to me that he could talk to her on the phone for hours and not be bored. She had a rich awareness of the other side. She was once in Nashville and had an Elvis experience. I have included her story in this book. She has the right to be validated for her ability and experiences.

As I watched her, I was in awe of her courage, and her ability to clearly state her fears and concerns about leaving the planet. She knew she might be dying, but she was giving it all that she had. I went to a meeting with her at the Wellness house, a place for people trying to heal cancer and other ailments. She belonged to a spiritual support group on Wednesdays. I was glad to go with her and support her. She needed people who could offer her a positive message about recovery. Joan was not concerned with herself, but she did want to heal and continue living. If she was dying, she wanted to have "a good death." I took that to mean that she would be at peace and not be afraid her transition to heaven.

Joan was concerned about herself, but was more concerned about her best friend, whom she feared wouldn't be able to make it alone after she passed. I promised I would help her friend, and try to counsel her after Joan's death. At first I asked myself if I should be promising her things I had no control over. I did so without fear, knowing it was the right thing to do for Joan. I just knew, and that was enough.

Please turn to page 90
for Joan's story

Chapter 7

Tools and Faith

Grief is the glue that makes us human. By sharing our grief with one another, we engage in the circle of life. As Billy Joel once said in one of his songs, "Life is a series of hellos and goodbyes. I'm afraid it's time for goodbye again." This is how the world works. When my mother passed away, my client called me up on the same day and said she had given birth to a son. This was in late December 1999. We buried my mother on New Year's Eve 1999. However, in March I found out that I was carrying a ten-week-old fetus inside me. My daughter was born healthy in November of 2000. She was a gift from my mother, and she came only after my mom left the planet.

In one year I went through the lowest low and then the highest high! I was forty-two years old when I gave birth to Sarah. Miracles do happen. Between the hellos and goodbyes, we have life. We have connection. We have moments that will never be forgotten. Everyone has peaks and valleys. Wholeness is more about how we feel and our attitude than a goal we try to achieve. How does letting go of grief help us to restore ourselves to our natural state of wholeness?

1. Letting go means we no longer obsess about the situation constantly.
2. Letting go means you can ask for help with the situation/ unknown results.
3. Letting go is a process that occurs over time/ as we learn to take responsibility for our lives.

4. Letting go helps us feel human and provides a release of negative energy.
5. Letting go means we turn our pain over to a higher authority to handle.
6. Letting go is believing we have choices and can take action on our own behalf.

By replacing victim thinking with survivor thinking, we avoid "learned helplessness."

One of my clients had a way of describing letting go with a horse analogy. When asked about her feelings for her husband, with whom she was not close to, she would say, "The horse has left the barn." She would go on to say that not only did the horse leave the barn, but also it was miles away and could no longer see the barn. This is how she felt. She had let go so much that she was not even connected to him in any significant way. She grieved the loss while she was still married, even though a child was involved.

She is now divorced, and yet she is waiting for her former spouse to leave the house. I wish that he would have left by now, but she has let go as much as she can. Sometimes we are letting go and still have transition issues beyond our control. I pray that one day soon, the house will be hers, and the former husband will find his place too.

I recently had a medium do a reading, and she told me that my mother wanted to come through. My mother was the type of woman who never held back her opinion. She was mad at my guides for always being the ones to talk to me. My guides simply moved back to let my mom speak.

Mom was furious with me for not taking care of myself. She said, "What about *you*?" She was worried that I put myself last in the taking-care-of department. I really do not maximize my good habits and build myself up. I exercise, but I don't drink enough water or eat enough protein. I have neglected myself by not buying new clothes or new shoes when the old ones get tight. I wear them anyway. I spent as little time as I can on my own appearance. My guides tell me I am pretty when I let myself be pretty. My mom told me from the other side that I have a long time to live, and I need to start now.

My dad also showed up in the reading. The medium asked me if my dad ever said he was sorry for the abuse I suffered as a child. My dad never said he was sorry or even admitted it to me. He is now in heaven. I was told that there are various levels in heaven. My dad had to go through a life review when he died, and he was placed on the lowest level of heaven. My husband says that he is in purgatory and must work on his sins to resolve them. I don't know if the lowest level in heaven is purgatory or not, but I do know he is not where my mother and brother are in terms of levels. They want to help him rise, but he must admit responsibility for his actions. His life review must have been brutal because he did bad things to people.

Forgiveness is the necessary ingredient on the way to health. Why berate myself for things I couldn't control? We can't go back and redo our history. We can only take the lesson we learned and try to use them to grow and mature. Some families I have seen have let jealousy and unresolved anger tear them apart. Some people don't realize that if the darkness is over you, you can do something about it. You don't have to blame anyone, you just start where you are. You don't have to live in a black hole. You can ask for help and get out of the hole. It's my responsibility to get out of the hole and to take control of my own life. I can be proactive, and let go of that grief and that role I played that almost destroyed me.

People think that grief magically disappears. I explain that grief just gets pushed down into our psyche and can manifest as a low-level depression. Whenever people have a loss, they should know that if you don't express it or acknowledge it, it gets caught up in a train of other unresolved grief. Therefore, this train gets carried around unnoticed by the person and has to be dealt with in one way or another.

Even if you replace the lost person, there are still residuals and denied parts. Most of the people I see have not resolved or properly grieved their losses. Many times these repressed feelings come out either in behavior or relationships. Hence, they come in for counseling and many times I see this baggage that gets carried around as unresolved grief.

Sometimes family members want those who have lost a loved one to "bounce back" and immediately do all the things that the first year requires. Some people can't even touch paperwork, books, taxes, or deal with the land that they owned together. It is normal to feel immobile at times, and the person has to do this when they feel emotionally ready.

This cannot be rushed, and people don't get back to their old selves so easily.

Many clients who have lost a spouse and have no children to help them are hit the hardest with overwhelming grief. Also, parents who have lost a child are hit the hardest because their lost child will never fulfill the dreams they created. Many feel betrayed and lonely.

We had a neighbor who died when she was hit by a car down the road. She had her children with her for a walk on a spring day. She had the baby in a harness and was pushing a baby carriage with her daughter in it. She also had the family dog along. It wasn't too long after she gave birth to her son that she felt good enough to go on a walk. I know that the little girl was a toddler.

A car came out of nowhere and hit her. The stroller made it to the other side of the street, but the little boy did not. I heard that some heroic person picked the child up and saved his life. The mother was not so lucky. The lady was in her thirties and was in the prime of her life. There was speculation that one car sideswiped another car and that was the car that hit her.

The whole neighborhood was stunned. The little boy only had minor injuries. I had friends who were at the scene, and it was chaos. The husband was beside himself. The children were traumatized, and it was devastating. The husband had the two children and left his company to take care of them. The lady's mother also watched the children. It was heartbreaking to pass their house and not want to hug them.

After the incident, they shut their door and never looked up to see who was around. They were devastated and rightly so. It was dark in the house for the longest time. They were in shock. I wrote them a letter about how sorry I was, and I would leave angels and cards at the door. For the first year the husband wouldn't even open the door. I don't blame them. They had a memorial up at the tree nearest to where she died.

I prayed and prayed for them. One day when I came to the door, the man opened the door a crack and took my offering. I was happy. They had the house up for sale, and yet no one would give them the price they were asking for. One day the door was open and the kids were playing outside. Something was changing. The man had Easter bunnies up on the windows and the family started to take more of an interest in the outside of the home. They were allowing themselves to heal.

Soon after that, they had a tent outside and a big party for one of the children. They looked up at people and spoke to us when we came to the door. I was so impressed with the family. They were coming back to life. It was great to see life again. The house was finally sold, and the family was able to move out of the house that was so painful to live in. The day I saw the moving van I felt joy and peace. The family went on to live in a new house. They took the memorial off the tree up the block and left the it bare.

If we let ourselves, we can move through the stages of grief. When they began to heal, they started to let the world in again. At the party, I heard laughter and celebration. I was an outsider looking in. All I know is that they moved and started a new life. The man put one foot in front of the other until he could release the darkness and rejoin the world. This is an example of how life continues and how people deal with the grief journey. I hope that wherever they are, they hold in their hearts the memories and the good times that they had with their lost loved one.

Chapter 8

Restoring Ourselves to Wholeness

With grief, we don't usually talk about restoration or wholeness because we will never get that person who died back. Are we forever cursed to a life devoid of our lost loved ones, in a cold, dark place without hope of a new life? I do know of a few things that are out there to help families heal from the loss, and reclaim their life. They manage to build in other realities, supports, and coping mechanisms. However, do we ever feel whole again? Can we ever be restored to our old normal, happy selves?

We need to have a "new normal," and since life goes on, how do we hold the memories of our loved ones? It depends on how you see recovery, and if you have family members to help you navigate the transitions. One gift that my neighbors had was a support system of friends and family that helped with the healing process. They did not do it alone.

All of this talk of restoration first came to me when I heard a popular evangelist on television talk about how God will restore us and make us whole after a loss. He is a very famous religious man who talks about how we can live our best life now. I thought about all the families that I have worked with over the years, and I came to understand just how hard this really is to do and to feel. My clients lost their twenty-two-year-old son and his twenty-two-year-old girlfriend on a December night after Christmas in a car accident. They have been moving forward for over ten years. They still have his room the same. Others have slept in it, and they have removed items and clothes from it for various reasons.

They have been involved in Bereaved Parents for over eleven years, helping other parents, having meetings at their home, and doing workshops. They have also hosted men's groups during conferences. These brave and courageous people have inspired me to enjoy my children and to enjoy life now. They still go to the crash site every year, have rituals on their son's birthdays, and have grown in this compassionate organization. I did workshops on life after death for the organization, and I marvel at their strength and commitment to grieving families.

I have to tell you that when another son got married a few years ago, they had a bridesmaid for their lost loved one. A bridesmaid walked alone in the wedding party signifying his absence, but they knew he was there in spirit. They also had something special at the wedding in memory of him. I was so touched. They may have done something unique, but the brother who lived wanted everyone at the wedding to know just how much his brother still meant to him. It didn't matter what anyone thought.

Prior to this wedding, one family picture they took was of the couple and the two children who were alive, while the mother held a framed picture of her deceased son taken at a baseball game. This family has been blessed in many ways. They have their daughter-in-law's birthday being the same date as the anniversary of their son's death. They need to celebrate life the same day they mourn their son's death. The son who was recently married had twins, a boy and a girl. So they lost two, but they got two grandkids. I see it as a sign from God that they were given two souls to nurture with the birth of the grandchildren. I recently heard that they are being blessed by the addition of another grandchild!

This has helped them with their grief by watching the children grow. Now they have a new experience with the other soon-to-arrive grandchild! My client's wife still does the newsletter for the organization, as it has changed since they first joined. The service they gave to others was so loving, and God continues to shine light on them. I learned that the group's energy helped each family heal in the way that was necessary for them to heal.

This letting go enables them to take a step back from the center of the pain, and move forward. They will always be devastated on one level, and grieve that their son who passed will never have a wife and kids, etc. It has been a long eleven years, but I admire them and feel honored to be a part of their healing journey. I so wish I could have known their son. At his old college, they have a baseball award every year in his name. The other players retired his baseball number, and he will continue to be missed by many. My client did have dreams about his son and his life on the other side.

His son tried to talk to him about what happened in the car crash, and tried to talk with him about heaven. His son has come to his dreams dressed differently than when he was waked. One time he had a baby with him, and my client was shocked. Can you really grow up in heaven? I know James Van Praagh has a new book by that very name. It is reported by many grieving parents that their lost loved one visits them in dreams, and no one has ever reported that a loved one is hurting or sick.

You can best believe that the after-death communication comes in funny and yet very specific ways. A lot of bereaved parents have had the son or daughter hug them in a dream. These dreams are real to the parents. Some of my clients have very touching conversations with their child on the other side. It has been a blessing, and it shows that the lost loved one knows how badly a parent needs her to make an appearance in a dream.

This after-death communication is across the board. You could want to hear from a spouse, friend, sibling, or parent, including grandparents. Who comes through is not promised. I was told by James Van Praagh that we don't get to pick who comes through. Whoever needs to come through, will come through. I asked him what it means when people who are not your family come through. He replied that it has something to do with forgiveness.

Going from earth to heaven is just like going through a door. I have had readings from a few mediums and one of them told me that my mother was shocked at how easy it was to cross over to the other side. Everything else was very hard for her to do. I wonder if they have cigarettes in heaven. When she was alive, she would choose cigarettes over anything.

My mother-in-law Agnes is a Catholic, and everyone knows that you will be sorry if you tell her that you didn't go to church on Sunday. She is very devout, but I found out that she has seen an angel going up to heaven when she was a child. She told me that she believes in reincarnation. I couldn't believe that she believed in that.

She told us that she had a dream about her son who died. This was my brother-in-law who had brain tumors and who died blind. She said that a few weeks after his death, she saw him in a dream. He had on his Marine garments and was leaning on a fence. Agnes said that he looked younger and in shape. She asked him, "Dave, are you all right?" He replied that he "guessed he was all right." She asked him if he had seen his father there.

Her husband died young of lung cancer. She said that he didn't speak, but that he showed her thousands of people's heads in front of him. Agnes thought that it meant that there were too many people there, preventing him from seeing his father. Even if that were true, his father might have been with the crowd. Dave seemed like he was out of it. It might be that heaven is crowded, but it might mean what Dan Piper, who wrote *90 Minutes in Heaven*, was talking about in his book.

In the book, Piper was welcomed to heaven. He reports seeing a sea of people, and people came from the back of the crowd to greet him. Were the heads Agnes saw the crowds of people who came to welcome Dave to heaven's gate? Was Dave confused about where he was, and why did he feel separated from the others there? This dream is very interesting because if Dave saw his father, Agnes might get a vision of him as well. I sure hope Dave and his dad are finally able to talk and share. I hope Dave accepted he was there and embraced those who came to heaven's gate to see him. The love of being embraced by beings of light must be beyond our comprehension.

Will we see our lost loved ones again? I believe that they never really left our side. Some of the signs they leave for their loved ones are amazing! Clients have reported that they tape old television episodes that their loved ones on earth can watch. They make lights go on or flicker, or they leave pictures of them out, and they even help us find items we are looking for! Sometimes they have a special number that keeps coming up, or a strange story to tell.

One client was with a male friend in Chicago recently. The waiter looked at them and asked if they were on a first date. They laughed, said no, and then the waiter said, "Did you meet at a funeral?" What? How did the waiter guess that they attended her husband's funeral a few months ago? Coincidence? I don't know, but it sounds far-fetched.

Not everything is a sign either. Sometimes your TV went out because of a power outage. Sometimes we just find a penny. If the signs help you, why not believe them? Nothing is for sure, but you can tell it's a sign if you get goose bumps, or if the energy seems out of the ordinary. Check yourself to see how you feel about the signs. Some people get freaked out and get scared. Others see it as comfort, and love getting them. This is of the spiritual realm.

To uncover the signs, one must be aware and observant. They usually center on dreams, things others say to you, and at the beginning of grieving, they will tell you that they are okay. I have enclosed a test I made up of different signs people have shared with me. Some have to do with intuition, some coincidences, and some that seem unreal. Are they real? You have to experience them and see if they ring true for you or not.

HAVE YOU HAD CONTACT WITH THE OTHER SIDE?

Check the experiences that you have had regarding your deceased loved one.

____ Found coins, medals or had money appear either at home or in public.

____ Lights or electricity going out or going on and no one touched them.

____ Musical toy or other musical objects suddenly start to play.

____ Pictures, objects, or money are moved from where you left them.

____ Someone is touching you, you feel someone's presence but no one is there.

____ You hear a loved one's voice, and no one is there.

____ You find notes, or cards are left out on the floor.

____ Some mass cards or pictures fall from where you put them.

____ You hear a deceased loved one's favorite song or a song you are touched by.

____ The microwave goes on at the same time a loved one used it in life.

____ People called and told you things that comforted you at that moment.

____ Coincidences with others—people you don't know share your experience.

____ Certain numbers keep popping up in strange places (deceased loved one's favorite).

____ Things the deceased ones said before their death suddenly make sense.

____ See TV shows or get articles, books, etc. that have meaning for you.

____ Dreams of your deceased loved one explaining what happened to them.

____ Dreams that show your loved ones in different clothes/cars/haircuts.

____ Dreams in which your loved one tries to talk with you about heaven.

____ Other people have dreams and give you a message from them.

____ Other people who have children were visited by your loved one.

____ You receive phone calls but no one is on the other end or you see that the number is coming from an office or old college number of the deceased.

____ You receive thoughts/dreams to call someone you haven't seen in years.

____ Your dog or cat behaves strangely or looks up and no one is there.

____ The clocks are changed/channels change on the TV with no one there.

____ You are doing a meditation and visualize your deceased loved ones.

____ Different smells (roses) or scents can be around you out of the blue.

____ Others _____

_____

_____

_____

If you have one or more checked, you have probably had spirit contact.

Forgiveness and Making Amends: The Healing Process

Forgiveness: Make space
Accept dark and light parts of you (embrace both)
Live in the now (power)
Release others (resentments)
Stop punishment (self-punishment/depression)

Defenses: Oldest and dearest friend
Inner child made sense of the world by creating these
- Survive attacks on self-esteem
- Ward off rejection/pain
- Fear of the unknown/lack of control
- Feelings of dependency and vulnerability

Self-Forgiveness: We are no better/no worse than others
Transform our lives (pain to love)
Resolution - no rage turned inward
Make honest assessment of strengths and weaknesses
Make amends to our inner child

Resistances to forgiving:
1. It hurts too much
2. Fears rejection or negative feedback
3. Likes to be "one up" on someone else
4. It's easier to blame someone else
5. Don't know what it means

False forgiveness:
1. Forgiving through forgetting
2. Forgiveness is offered, but there is much resentment
3. Forgiveness offered just to create peace
    Before understanding the damage done
    But the wrong is repeatedly brought up
    But someone else now "owes you"

Grief and Loss: How can I help?

As a culture we avoid death because it makes us uncomfortable. We don't know what to say or how to help. The unpleasant feelings hold us back from comforting the bereaved family. What can we do to help?

We are stronger when we share our story with others. By sharing our strength, hope, and prior experiences with others, we bond in unity.

The grieving process is a spiritual process. Our community can be a comfort and support to those experiencing a loss. Take care of yourself when working with grief and have a safe place to go to talk about your own concerns. Here are some ways to help others grieve:

- Show your support.
- Be available.
- Keep your promises.
- Avoid clichés ("it was her time," "time heals all wounds," etc.).
- Be honest ("let me know what I can do to help you").
- Avoid judgments and comparisons.
- Remember that the grief process has no limit or time frame.
- Remember significant dates/anniversaries.
- Be a good listener. Grief takes time and has many emotions.

Stages of Grief: The person does not need to do these in order.

1. Shock, Denial
2. Anger   The difference between grief and
3. Bargaining   depression: grief has no need to
4. Depression   self-harm.
5. Acceptance

Tasks of Mourning

1. Accept the reality of the loss.
2. Work through the pain of grieving.
3. Adjust to the environment without the person.
4. Withdraw emotional energy from the deceased (move, make new friends).
5. Deal with reawakening of past unresolved losses.

The Forgiveness and Restoration to Wholeness

What do we do to forgive ourselves for what we did or didn't do for our lost loved one? I believe that the forgiveness of self is essential in any grief process. With self-forgiveness, we let go of guilt and/or shame, actions, or inactions on our part in relation to the grief journey. Some people feel guilty even when they did everything right. Many times we blame ourselves for things that were not in our control in the first place. Sometimes people die when their loved ones take a vacation.

I remember a family who had taken care of their father for many months in a row. They needed the time to relax and recharge. They felt so guilty that they were not there when he passed. Did anyone ever think that perhaps our lost loved ones wait for their family to leave before they die? Some loved ones don't want us at the deathbed. In other families, spouses and mothers have been out of the room, or even in the bathroom when their loved one passed.

Do our loved ones become whole again after they die? Most people I have heard believe that on the other side, we are whole and productive. Spiritual medium Cindi Muntz, whose quote is on the back cover, believes that they return to wholeness after death. But what about the person who feels responsible for the death, what happens to that person?

We are never the same after a loss. We can live through the wake and funeral. Many wonder if they can do what it takes to survive. Many clients that I have seen don't remember the time after a death. Some people know they are working in a diminished capacity, but they keep working because they have to. Other clients of mine are facing financial problems at the same time when dealing with a loss. The depression hits every family. People feel like they are in a dream, a daze, or are just exhausted. The task of rebuilding lives comes later. For the moment, just sleeping through the night is a welcome relief.

The secret to healing from loss is to believe that you can recover. Loss is like the dark night of the soul—you must go through it, and you can't get around it. By being committed to recover, we are not victims but survivors. It's okay to be present with others and express all of our feelings.

Many times families get together and help the survivors. I have seen and heard how families came together when someone passes. I have also seen how a death can tear families apart. People can be really petty about money and items they may want from the estate. There may also be jealousy between the executor and other relatives, and issues on how relatives feel about what was left to them. It can go either to the negative or positive way. It's our choice.

Most people ask me on a daily basis, "How do I live without my lost loved one?" Most people have no idea, and they are terrified. I usually say "one day at a time" and by putting one foot in front of the other. They may feel lost at first.

Do you know that the true purpose and meaning of our lives is being able to be receptive to our innermost self? Wholeness means that we accept and value parts of ourselves that hide who we are—even from ourselves. Remember earlier when I said I was afraid of the light? I didn't want anyone to see the parts of me that were confused, weak, sad, and angry.

Growing spiritually and changing our habits and thoughts begin with being able to invite the unknown parts of us to emerge. Trusting ourselves and knowing who we are gives us a spiritual foundation for our lives. It is wise to journal after a loss, to see what issues come up for you. Be courageous and look inside yourself. Grief therapy helps to cope with the aftermath of the death.

When the parts accept themselves, the more people heal. There is a popular song by John Legend, and part of the lyrics say, "I give you all of me, you give me all of you. Love your curves and all your edges, all your perfect imperfections." This is what we hope to accomplish in this life. Embracing all parts of us helps us to heal and grow. Pushing past the uncomfortable feelings and anxiety, we share our hopes, dreams, and experiences with others. When we truly love all parts of our self, we are whole. We understand now why we have certain defenses or habits. We accept that we need to have a plan of action to rebuild our lives.

We can feel compassion for the parts of us that have sat in the darkness, isolation, and fear for years. Perhaps your lost loved one knew about some parts of you that you didn't share with the world. If that is true, then your connection with your lost loved one was one of acceptance and unconditional love.

I have heard from some widows that their marriages were deep expressions of the soul. Many people don't realize it, but the bond people may have had with their spouses, children, friends, and neighbors were real soul connections. These connections never die. I have also heard that the more you loved someone, the more you grieve. The fact that you had this capacity to love is forever in your heart. Rejoice in the knowledge that the divine lives in you. Your spirit is like a light that never goes out. We all have our light, and if we love ourselves fully, we can grow after the death of a loved one.

Grief recovery is not steady. It's more like a wind that goes around in circles. It is just a process that is very painful. Many of the families that I have worked with are devastated and cannot function after the death of a parent or spouse. They become depressed and spend many isolating nights by themselves.

In the first few months, people stay busy and surround themselves with friends to distract them from the reality of the death. In some ways this is very comforting. Grief hits people at any time of the day or night. It's like a door opens and the grief falls out. Some people still cry every day after a year or more. That's why a support group is essential for people experiencing a loss.

In a group setting, people help one another. They empathize with the feelings others have, and have a new place to grow. You would never think that a funeral home could be a source of comfort, but it can. Sometimes we forget that the meeting is being held in the casket room. Unless there is a funeral going on when we are there, we hardly ever remember where we are. This holds true for me. At other times go out to dinner as a group or share items that were important to our lost loved one. Here are some tips from these groups:

1. Have hope and believe that you are going to recover. It will be up and down, especially for those who were very close to their spouse, parent, sibling, or child—even adult children. It's a mindset that propels us forward.
2. Please allow all your feelings to come to light especially anger against God, the hospital, your lost loved one, etc. Anger is a crucial part of recovery, so share your anger with the group. Anger is energy, and anger turned inward is depression. Some people go between anger and depression and sadness in a cycle.
3. Don't be afraid of your lost loved one if you feel their presence or get a "sign" from heaven that they are all right. Don't ask them to get in bed with you if you are terrified. These are some experiences people ask for, but if you are scared and anxious, it won't be a positive experience.

4. Ask for signs that involve less intense validation, like asking for a feather, pennies, or turning the lights on or off. It is alleged that the spirits on the other side can manipulate electricity, and your phone can ring with no data on the caller ID. This has happened a lot to me, sometimes when I am actually in session with their loved one in therapy! One lady lost her boyfriend and father. She asked the dad to flicker the Christmas lights on the tree (she had it up all year long). She asked frequently too. If you don't believe in signs, that's perfectly fine too.

When we feel whole, we know that the emptiness inside of us is real, but it is filled with hope rather than despair. Many people look to other people to fill them up, but God is the only one who can fill that hole inside of us. When you let go, you are relinquishing your will and surrendering over to the divine. You start to see obstacles move out of your way, or an energy change. Insights and clarity come to your mind, and you begin to relax and know that God is there. God gives us what we need, not what we want. Knowing that you are safe and in the arms of the angels brings a sense of peace. This may not happen all the time. When you feel the calmness and think clearly, you can be a help to others as well as to yourself. Your energy changes.

I had the honor of knowing a great man, an ex-priest and healer who was touched by God and who led a spiritual community in the 1980s and 1990s. He was a gifted and a powerful healer. He helped thousands of people and was very popular. His name was Ron Roth. He did healing masses, and even I was touched by his love.

I remember being in a healing ceremony and in my mind's eye, I saw a baby on a rug. I was confused because I had severe endometriosis, and was told that I was infertile. That's why we adopted. However, this baby was clear as day to me. When I was forty-two, I had this baby. It actually manifested. This was a miracle of God, because if I listened to the infertility experts, they told me I had a 3 percent chance of actually having a baby using modern infertility procedures. They said I would never conceive.

This great man told this huge group that one day he was unhappy doing his duties as a priest. The parish needed so much, and he was tired. He knew the lady whose home he was visiting that day was hard to handle, needy, and very longwinded. He said that God told him to just show up at the appointment, and God would do the rest. He was very resentful, but he followed his orders. At the end of the meeting, she gave him needed food, money, and other goods for the church. He told us to just show up at your appointments and God will get you what you need. That's how we can begin to get taken care of by God and his angels.

When looking at gifts of the spirit, remember that the gift comes when you least expect it. We are not going to demand gifts, but simply do good deeds and be kind to others. The more we give, the more we receive. All we have to do is ask God for help, turn the problem over to him, and see what happens. If you are living in the moment, any day can be awesome. You need to think that God will be there, and feel positive feelings toward yourself and others. This needs to be learned.

Be careful not to listen to negative tapes in our mind that stop us from feeling good. Don't get stuck in the darkness. Darkness manifests as self-doubt, self-criticism, and judging yourself and others. Be careful whose energy is around you. If the people or places are negative, you can lose your light. It's better to write a gratitude journal, and write down any spiritual happenings daily. If you look for positive signs that God is with you, you protect yourself, and live in the now. Now is all we have, and we are empowered by not living in the past or the future.

Living in the Light

When dealing with love, soul connections and loss, we are dealing with the energy flow of the universe. All things must change over time, and if not, we hold the flow of life away from us in a rigid, controlling way. In our rigid mindset, we avoid change and loss. We cannot control the death experience. We never know when it's our time to leave, so we protect ourselves from the truth that all living things die. The anxiety of that reality is overwhelming. We never know how long we will have a person. We have a hard time talking about death and dying, and we rarely discuss the situation with our loved ones

When someone close to us dies, we are left with a big gaping hole in our soul and in our life. We literally ache for them to return, and the more years spent with the person, the more distraught the survivor is. We try to distract ourselves from the reality of the situation. We deny the truth and pretend the person will be home soon. Don't be upset if you do this. This is our mind trying to protect us from the impact of the loss. Denial is unconscious, you don't even know you are in it. We try to adjust to life without the loved one, but it gets overwhelming.

If we get stuck in the pain and loss, we cannot fire up enough energy to start and rebuild our life. Whatever we build after the death, it can never be the same again. We build a "new normal," and try to act in positive ways. Some people feel a part of them has died with the lost loved one. Some have rituals daily that keeps them close to their loved one, like going to visit them where they are buried.

Some people have a shrine or altar to the deceased. Others have their loved ones' ashes in a nice container in their homes. There is no wrong or right. You do what is helpful to you. Some join grief support groups. They realize they need to feel strong to get "through" the first year. I like to ask each person how he or she envisions his or her future life. Some people and families can't even go there emotionally. They simply ask how they are going to live without their lost loved one. Many are distraught because there is no correct way to go on.

I went to see psychic medium James Van Praagh when he started to emerge as a medium with his books. He said that there is no pain when we die. He told us that those who have crossed over are fine, and that they don't want their loved ones living a dead life. They want their loved ones here to go on with their life. We were at a beautiful venue filled with almost two thousand people. We all came to connect to our loved ones. Everyone was sending messages to him saying, "Pick me." We all wanted "to get" a reading. He told us that thinking that way did not help the process.

We were really there for ourselves. We all wanted to hear from the other side. We miss our lost loved ones. He couldn't read everyone. He asked us to think about the big picture, and those that he brought through had common themes we all could relate to. If you ever see a medium at a big venue, realize that the chances are that your lost loved one will not come through. Some people are distraught, but try to remember that these venues are for group healings.

These souls came in to teach us, and to model for us. Everyone was amazed to see who did come through, and the group experience was that we all had these losses. We all know someone who took their life. We all had "stubborn" fathers and mothers, and relatives we could not get through to. We were there to help the greater good for all those who suffer from grief. Many were disappointed their loved one didn't come through, but the group experience was the thing that fostered the healing among all the people gathered there.

The dead are not dead. They are still connected by the love bonds between you and them. This world of thoughts is important, because we need to have hope that we can survive and thrive after they leave us. Lots of people suffer in silence after a tragedy. You have no idea how many people cannot accept help even when they are so close to telling their story. Many people have had this experience, but never open up. Many stay frozen in the old feelings, and just by attending a workshop or lecture, they open up the pain they have hidden deep inside of them.

Remember that if you can't feel the pain, you can't feel the joy. If our feelings are repressed or frozen or hidden away, it is harder to live a joyful life. We hold our grief in, but it comes out in ways we cannot know beforehand. Some people think that these feelings go away, but they don't. They eat away at the person concealing them. They spend lots of energy trying to remain hidden. But they come out in our relationships or leak out when you least expect them to.

Why not allow the feelings to come up, and release them. People think that if they cry once, they won't be able to stop. The same with anger or sadness. We have to find ways to let go of the pain, and transform that pain to power. When we share our grief in a public way, we all learn. That's why we are on this earth. Our soul heals from the exposure of our secrets, doubts, insecurities, and anger.

Just remember that your lost loved ones want you to go forward, and have a life. They want you to laugh. They may have even sent you another person who you could love. Take very good care of yourself. Heaven can wait for you. I am amazed at how those who have lost someone can come back into life and live again. Please allow yourself to have fun, and feel all your feelings—the good, the bad, and the ugly. Feelings aren't good or bad, they are just feelings.

Talk about your wishes with your loved ones while you are alive. Don't be afraid to educate yourself about grief. Let's talk about the elephant in the room, especially if someone is terminally ill. It's okay to talk to your loved one about death. Most people want to have a "good" death. They are better equipped with the transition when they have all their papers in order.

Grief is a part of life, and we can find help and peace. This is our school on earth. Your soul learns what it came here to learn. Don't be afraid of death, be afraid of a life not lived to its fullest. My heart goes out to grieving people and families. I am sending love, light, and peace to you all. May this book be a testimony to how love never dies. Love is never wasted. A priest told me years ago, "Never let human experience destroy you." There is always hope for healing.

We are all going to die. Why not tell the truth about death. People have died way before they should have. Young, healthy people die. Untimely death leads to confusion and fear. Instead of repressing this fact, we can face it. Once we face that we will not always have the person next to us, we can be open to growth. When we have a loss, we must reinvent ourselves without that support. We can die holding onto the memory of our lost loved one, and some people do die of a broken heart. I would like to see people reinvest slowly into a new life.

The process is long, and the emptiness lingers. I see your courage to go on, and I admire you. We need each other to support this new normal. It's the difference between heaven and hell. In hell, no one helps each other. They have to eat with long sticks and they become frustrated. In heaven, people eat with long sticks. They can't reach their mouths without help. The secret is that they all feed each other. Be an angel to another grieving person, and feed each other. Giving up the ghost means that we focus on the support of our earth angels. We can't do it alone. Don't stay in darkness and isolation.

Anybody can help just by smiling at us. Reach out and help another person. Embrace them, comfort them, and pass along all the wisdom you learned. The angels in heaven rejoice too. We are all spirits waiting to go home. When earth school is over, we will see our lost loved ones again. The light will be shining, and the path illuminated so we go the right way. Our lost loved ones or angels will lead us there.

Don't let grief rob you of your life. I know that it can be hard to enjoy life. For many years I lived a "dead" life. I didn't enjoy every day. It took me years to grieve my losses, and I am not afraid to tell the truth. I have a hard time letting go and releasing the past. I can get messages from the other side, but I need to reach out and accept the fact that I am still on earth for a reason. I can live my dreams and teach my clients and children the joy of living in the present. We teach what we most need to learn.

Let's help ourselves, our neighbors, and friends heal and grow from loss. We can embrace a grieving person and fly with them toward a rainbow. On the way to brighter days, we can navigate and help them avoid the despair and dark clouds. We have a choice. Remember, our lost loved ones want us to move on. They have a hard time with the suffering they see their families go through. There are good things that come out of the darkness. We get to see how much love we felt for our lost loved one.

One man on the other side told his wife to move on. She was not ready. He told her to at least throw away his toothbrush. Can you believe how hard it was for this spouse to throw out the toothbrush? It was so hard for her. This was after almost a year since he died. She still is upset that he wanted her to move on. He also said that he checked out who she should be with as her new husband. She was not impressed. She passed on the choice. I can't make her move forward either. This man hated his wife being so sad.

I watched an old show from the year 2000 on The Oprah Winfrey Network (OWN) the other day on forgiveness. They had a rabbi there to help a mother who had a horrible experience and lost her son in a freak accident. She didn't know how to start to forgive herself. The first step was to tell others her story of loss. The second is that we need to remember that we are human. He was urging her to start having a life again. Moral people feel guilt, so that's not bad, he said. He told her that this was her beginning to heal herself.

It was a touching show. How many people think that they are the reason their loved ones died? They didn't do this right, or they didn't stay overnight to watch over them, etc. Please realize that maybe that wouldn't have stopped the event from happening. One lady who lost her only daughter said that she dreamed that her daughter was going to die. The next day, it became a reality. Even my own dad was told in a dream that my brother would die within the year. He didn't believe it, but it was true. You can see someone alive the day before, and the next day they can be gone. For all of us, it is too hard to understand how easy they can go from one state of being to being dead.

Remember, if you loved with your whole heart, you won't feel complete or whole again until you let go, release that person, and stop taking responsibility for their passing. Death is easy compared to living each day trying to save the ones we love from the death experience. When they leave the earth, I am told that it is like going through another door. A trusted medium once told me that my own mom was surprised how easy death was compared to life. Everything had been hard for her except crossing over.

Love yourself and honor those who have passed. Restoration is possible, but it can never be the same again. Can we rise to the challenge that grief provides us as human beings? It's all in the way you think. Think peace, think love, and think restoration of your soul. Think good thoughts. What you think about expands in your mind and helps free you from pain and suffering.

Sometimes people hold onto old problems because it gives them a purpose or a mission. However, we get no paybacks and we can't go back and have the past behavior change into what we would have liked it to be. We must move out of the fear and anger and into a place of surrender. Yes, it happened. Yes, we were hurt. Yes, it colored all of our relationships and affected our self-esteem. We can never get it back. What we do have is the divine, and God's promise to help us create a new life. I have seen people who have turned over their lives and their wills to God get blessings, opportunities, and friends just by releasing old patterns and asking God to help them create new lives.

What do we have to lose? If you suffer from an addiction, get help. Recovery from grief is beautiful. Not every day, but some of the time. Open your hearts to the light. Ask for help, and love yourself despite all your imperfections. Be human.

Epilogue

When dealing with love, connection, and loss, we are dealing directly with the energy of the universe. All living things die, including all of us. The time that we have on earth is only a blink of an eye in terms of eternity. We come here to learn, and our mission is to further the soul in its development. Some souls choose a very difficult time on earth, while others seem to have it easy. Everyone is touched by sorrow just because we all must experience the sting and the pain of losing someone close to you. In later years, older people continue to face losses of their families, friends, neighbors, and coworkers. Even strangers' deaths can touch them by association. I knew some of my college friends died in 9/11. I didn't really know them, but I grieved for them anyway.

When someone close to us dies, we ache for them to return, trying to distract ourselves from the reality and the finality of death. We use other coping mechanisms to help us function as we begin the tasks of mourning. We go through stages of grief, and we are in shock, especially in the beginning.

The one stage that many are afraid of is the anger phase. People who are usually nonemotional go through this phase confused. I have told people that when you let go of the anger, you are making peace with your heart. The heart opens and there is more space inside of you to heal and to move to another level. One person started to want to avoid the people that helped her to get through in the beginning time period of the death. She felt badly, but she wanted to start with new people without the reminder of the pain. This is normal, and nothing to feel badly about. This is a sign of growth.

Some people are capable of insight, and realize that they want to start fresh with new friends not connected to the loss and grief. This is not selfish, this means that you want to move forward. One client of mine was able to recognize this and brought it up as a problem. Sometimes people just need some space and permission to go places without their supportive grief helpers. They don't have to cut these people out of their lives. They are healing and are trying to integrate new experiences, and new people who might not be aware of the recent loss issues.

Giving up the ghost is really about giving up our fear about the future. Giving up the ghost allows us to live in the present and to continue with life despite the pain. If we stand up to fear, we can remember the love that was there and enable ourselves to honor that person while we are still alive. If we don't live in fear, we can trust in God that he will take care of us. I have had to do this in my life. I have to trust that my God or higher power will help me recover. We can't do it alone. We should allow ourselves to feel our feelings, and then engage in life again.

The process by which we are ready to give up the ghost is a long and hard struggle. By letting go and letting God work in your life, you are given the tools to help yourself. It's as if you become free of the burden of loss. When the soul leaves the body, it is free to float and glide in other dimensions. When you give up the fear and let go of the grief, it frees up your energy to invest in the world around you again. It is like being reborn.

I wish everyone who is grieving knows that our soul and our essence are divine. We experience our divinity as being a peaceful and loving part of us. I wish all of you the peace and the ability to grow from the grief experience. We see what we learned from the process of grieving, and with every goodbye, we learn something about ourselves and the world. We are healed by our faith and by the community, which we embrace during the most difficult part of our lives.

I have witnessed that when the funeral is going on, the love of family and friends can be very soothing, and very supportive. However, when the reality sets in, those people go away and go back to their lives. We may pause for those few days to show our grief, but people don't realize that the loneliness still persists. The people in the family are for the most part left alone, needing help more than anyone knows. We simply put it behind us and get back to life. What about those families who are hurting and still need support?

My grief group has some widows who were very close to their spouses and had no children. These ladies and men may live alone in a big house, and stay isolated, especially during winter months. Some of the women don't drive, and they might suffer from depression already. The mind can sink into depression so easily, and many nights sleep is lost because they ache for their lost spouses. I had a man in the group who was married over forty years. We thought we were going to lose him after his wife died. However, a few years later he actually met another widow and they are now together. It was great to see him happy and enrolled in life again. He was finally able to accept that his wife was gone. It happened in his time, and he let go when he felt ready to do so.

No one should rush you to grieve. You grieve in your own time and in your own way. There is no time limit. Just be aware of getting stuck in the grief and doing self-harm to yourself. If you are hurting yourself, please get help. Your lost loved one does not want you to cause any harm to yourself. If you are stuck in depression and need help, contact your local mental health center or hospital for referrals to grief counselors or groups that can help you sort out your feelings.

I have often heard that time heals all wounds. That is not true. Time does not heal the wound. It is what you are doing with the time that helps heal the wound. If we use that time after the death to get involved in life again, we will slowly heal. We are forever changed by loss. We need each other. We need loving kindness and a friend to talk to. You are not bothering people by asking them to help you. You have my permission to ask for help from a neighbor or a friend.

We all want peace and harmony. I wish all of you this peace. Go slowly and gently on the healing journey. Take care of yourself and the ones you love. Your soul already knows this peace. Meditate and listen to the silence. It speaks the truth.

You can heal. I hope this book helps you by validating what you most need to hear. Choose to live in the light, not the darkness. If you tend to isolate, reach out instead of being alone. Remember the angels are with us, and your lost loved ones are safe in heaven. Don't let fear stop you from going forward. Ask God to take away the fear that stops you from moving forward with your life. You are not alone. I would love to hear from you about your grief journey. Never give up.

Here is a quote from Rabbi Nachman of Breslov, who was born in 1772 in the Ukrainian village of Meddzeboz. He was the great-grandson of the Baal Shem Tov, founder of the Hasidic movement. In his book *The Empty Chair: Finding Hope and Joy,* he spoke of healing, wholeness, and of being alive! In his lifetime he attained outstanding levels of righteousness and wisdom. He is an inspiration to me because he spoke to people in an honest and sincere way. His teachings are more for this time period, rather than in the 1800s.

He died in 1810 at the age of thirty-eight. Rabbi Nachman told his followers that his influence and light would endure long afterward. He is my guide and "project manager" in the spirit. He believes in mastery over pain and suffering and overcoming obstacles. He wants us to talk out loud to God and pour out our hearts to our creator. He wants us to think positive. Here is some of his wisdom:

Peace heals. When your own world is fractured, increase your knowledge of God. It will spawn inner peace. When the outside world is fractured, promote the search for truth. It will spawn universal peace.

I want you all to know that anyone can pray to Rabbi Nachman and my rabbi guides if they need help. My guides have led me out of some very dark places in my heart and soul. We should all help one another and pray for those in need. Rabbi Nachman states that in life we walk on a narrow bridge, and the most important part is to not be afraid. I wish you all courage and strength to heal. The Kabbalah Center has classes and books and a new way to look at life. If your soul is searching for wholeness and spiritual growth, consider studying Kabbalah. The light will help heal you.

Just know that by healing, you help heal the world as well. We are all connected by the light and love of God. We only have one life to live. Enjoy each day and know that you will be united with your lost loved one when it is time. For now, help others and love and accept yourself. Ask for angelic and divine guidance. As my husband always tells me, "If you don't ask, you don't get!"

Doreen Virtue, who writes all the time about angels, was in Chicago a few years ago, and I went to her workshop. There had to be close to one thousand people there! She told us, "Don't talk to me about your concerns unless you have asked your angels for help and guidance first." It's okay to both ask for help and receive help. Remember, with every goodbye, we learn.

Before my brother Michael died, he sent me all of his pots, pans, and kitchenware. I did not know why he sent me all of that. When he died a week later, I realized what he was saying. He wanted me to live in his place, and use his things and carry on. He knew he was going to die, so he cleaned house, so to speak. My brother was very spiritual, and wanted me to continue to live. His last words to me were, "Karen, we have to forgive." I thought to myself, "Forgive what?" I had no idea what he meant.

The next day my dad called and said that Michael was dead. When he told me that a van had run over him, I realized that he was talking about forgiving the driver of that van for hitting him. The driver fled the scene and was never found. Years later my dad had a reading over the phone with psychic Sylvia Browne. He asked if the person who hit my brother felt bad or had guilt for running him over and for fleeing the scene. Sylvia said, "No, he doesn't feel bad at all." This upset my dad, and then Sylvia told him that the driver moved to Florida and would never be connected to the crime.

My brother told us to bury him with my mother if he died. That's what we did. He tells me that he has plenty of girlfriends and is fine. He told me that my mother came to take him to heaven. He said he didn't feel any pain. His soul was out of his body just before the van hit him. I believe that no soul goes through the death transition by itself.

In summary, we are spiritual beings having a human experience. I remember when John Bradshaw first talked about the family as a system. He was a recovering alcoholic, and used the twelve-step program to heal his addictions. I read somewhere that the people who make amends to others and work the program are able to let go and forgive themselves. Some people live with many regrets and other resentments they don't let go of. My message is to forgive yourself and others for things you could not control. Don't be a prisoner in your own prison. You have the key to free yourself.

Remember that the earth is the school, and that heaven is our true home. As the soul awakens after the death transitions, it often finds itself surrounded by people whom the soul knew and loved on earth. Dan Piper's book *90 Minutes in Heaven* says the same thing about the people who greet us as we enter into heaven.

The doorway to death is just that—a doorway. In the book, *The Place We Call Home*, the author explains why we are here.

We are souls following a magnificent journey through the material world, on a quest to learn to love more fully and deeply and to relinquish our fears and the illusions of our limitations. We are spirit beings, eternal, divine, and endless. The love that we realize, manifest, and give to others while on earth will light the path through and beyond this world, beyond the valley of the shadow, to a place in spirit where we came, the place from where all love and light emanate, the place we call home. (p. 197–8)

I hope this book helps you to see where you are in terms of dealing with death and loss. We don't have unlimited time. Let's be angels to one another, and try not to be critical or compare how different people grieve. The restoration in our lives takes time. By reading this book, you have already started the process.

I wish you complete healing. That means that you have chosen to walk forward on the path of life. By remembering our lost loved one, we hold them dearly in our heart, and honor them in a way that you know they would like. Some people have planted trees; some helped specific charities, helped others, or simply lived the life that their loved one would have been proud of. Know that you will see them again. My cousin, who is over eighty-five, told her husband who is up in heaven, "I'm not ready to come yet! I have grandchildren and great-grandchildren!" She will come eventually. Until then, she is engaged in and loving her life! I wish you the same joy!

This letter was written by a 25-year-old man who dies in bed of an epileptic episode. He dictated this letter to his stepdad while the stepdad was at the computer. HE writes of heaven and how we will still be connected to his family. Since his death was sudden, they tried to make sense out of his words.

This Place

November 1996
(your calendar)

Dear Mom, Dad, Tricia, Ashley, and all of the rest of you who are thinking of me,

This letter is to let you know how I am doing, and how I feel about being here!

I have been getting all of your letters, and I want you to know I appreciate all the thoughts that all of you have been sending my way. I know all of you have been wondering if I can know the things you have been thinking, writing, and talking to each other about me. The simple answer to that question is YES.

This is such a strange place compared to where you guys spend your time. It is not really possible for me to describe this place to you in a form that you would understand, other than to say that you will all love it here when your turn comes to join me.

Ha ha, I already know when that will be, but of course, I cannot tell you now.

The strangest thing about this place is that I don't really miss you guys, because I am able to be with you any time I want, simply by thinking that I want to be with you.

Isn't that something? And even stranger is the fact that any time you talk or think about me, I am called to your attention, no matter what I happen to be doing.

And please believe me, there is no end of wonderful things to do––all the "time." ("Time" is a concept that doesn't apply to this place, and I never have to waste "time" with things like eating or sleeping––unless I want to eat or sleep.)

Everybody––please don't feel sorry for me. I really do love this place. The thing I feel bad about is you guys are locking in your "time" and I know you all are suffering because I am gone. You keep saying things like "Christmas won't be the same without Erik" and "Erik will never be able to watch Kendell grow up to be a woman" and "I wish Erik was here to do this with us 'cause he would love it," etc.

Surprise, guys. I will be there at Christmas; I will watch Kendell grow; and every time you go to Target, Ashley, I can go with you if I want. Maybe you guys can't see me or hear me, but some of those thoughts you are having come from me!

Mom, I know how you are feeling. Please don't feel a loss over me. I am with you any time you want me, and please know I am in a good place.

Please tell Stacy that I can see good things are going to happen for her. I know how hard it was for her to be the one who had to find my body. And I am delighted that you guys have taken her in. She is a great kid.

Tell Michele and company that Katherine Legge is the perfect place to plant that tree. I am very joyed to visit you guys there. And the perfect spot for me to watch the kids in the winter.

Dad, I know you are sad about our modeling. I hope you will continue to build, especially your jet, but if you want to wait awhile, it is okay. Go out to the field and maybe you'll get the bug again.

Oh yeah. Dad, forget about John. He is just being himself.

Tricia, you are going to have a great future. Hang in there, and everything will be fine.

I love all of you, and I know you are thinking of me all the time.

Love,
Erik

In the Country Music Hall of Fame
by Joan Luckey

Before I get into this amazing adventure, let me start by telling you that most of my encounters with spirits happened when I least expected it. This occasion was no exception. I am clairaudient. Walk with me through the Country Music Hall of Fame and experience the awesome presence of Elvis and other music greats.

The date was February 23, 2005. I was visiting with family in Nashville, with my friend, Art. Having time to check out only one of Nashville's main attractions, Art and I decided to visit the Country Music Hall of Fame. Although neither of us were heavy into country music, there were enough country singers on both our lists of favorites that we reasoned it would be a memorable experience. Besides, there are so many great country singers that crossed genre into blues, jazz, rock, etc. We expected much to keep us occupied. Little did I imagine how extraordinary this choice would turn out to be.

The outside architecture of the museum exhibits the form of a keyboard, with the windows representing the black keys. The musical staff surrounds a circular adjoining building. From the very first steps down the sidewalk approaching the museum, I felt a peacefulness and sense that this was a special place.

Entering the Country Music Hall of Fame near the ticket counter, we stopped momentarily to take in a quick look at the expansive hall. We could make out a gift shop on the other end, eateries, and space in between that surely was the site for many musical entertainment events. Knowing we would be checking this all out later, we approached to purchase our tickets and were directed down a short hall to an elevator. A pleasant person welcomed us and oriented us to the experience we were about to have.

An elevator door opened and we were taken to the third floor to a cathedral-ceiling-high room, with the walls covered with huge posters of artists. This was the beginning. We were instructed to take our time enjoying the exhibits, and to simply keep moving forward, working our way around and down to the first floor.

Following this entranceway began glass case displays full of personal effects of artists, their clothes, instruments, and many other interesting items. Associated with each one was a small story of the artist and the item. We were able to press a button and hear samplings of their songs. Occasionally we were given the history of the writing of the song itself.

We entered booths where we listened to songs of some artists. The use of sound in the museum was impressive. When you stood in front of an exhibit, or in a booth, you could hear the music or audio review clearly, yet someone just feet away from you is not disturbed, and hears only what is in front or above them!

Because I did not bring my reading glasses with me, I tended to spend more time taking in the artifacts and audio offerings. Art did much more reading. His time with each exhibit tended therefore to be longer, and he would fall behind me. Every now and then I would wait and we'd get caught up in absorbing something together. A member of the staff occasionally also joined in and shared even more interesting insights.

As I feel the spirits moving me to get on with the meat of the story—their store, I will not delve in further details of the museum's many exhibits, except to encourage everyone who can to come to experience the museum for themselves.

As Art proceeded to get absorbed in an exhibit, I proceeded on the Elvis's Gold Cadillac. Waiting for Art to catch up, I passed time taking in the detail of the car. The passenger doors were open, so I could see in. I marveled at the full bar and TV, quite impressive items in those days. I began thinking of Elvis actually using this vehicle, and how many exciting, happy, and fun times must have been had. I started fantasizing seeing him and his buddies getting into the car, carousing, and laughing the day or evening away.

It was then that I felt a wave come over me, that I recognized as spirit attempting communication. It was like I had entered another dimension. I was in the hall, but some part of me was elsewhere. I have had experiences like this all my life. Still, I rarely seek it out, and it is rare to happen. It was nowhere on my mind this day.

I settled into this space of mental quietness, and waited. Then it came:

"I am here!"

"Who?" I asked.

"Elvis."

Oh my, you can imagine my amazement. I scoffed at myself that this must be my mind playing tricks on me.

"Elvis? Elvis is really here?"

"I am. Yes."

My stomach sank as I absorbed the possible reality of what I was hearing. Mind you, the conversation was in my mind. My first impression was to discard it as imagination. Even though skeptical, I replied:

"Elvis, *you* are really here?"

"Yes, I *am* here!"

Yeah, sure, I thought. I still wasn't buying it. I told myself my mind was playing tricks on me, some imaginative wishful thinking. Even though I have had contacts with spirits before, they were few in number and almost always when I wasn't trying.

"*I am here!*" I heard with emphasis. "There are others."

He spoke in that deep, rich, resonant, and distinctive voice that is all so familiar, often imitated but never really duplicated.

"All right, okay, hmmmm, well . . ." I didn't know what to do or say at this point. Art then appeared at my side, both of us leaning on a rail. I focused away from the ethereal.

"Cool," he said. He pointed out the little chips and dents you could see on the car and door.

"Look, that's from Elvis closing his door." We bantered some imaginative stories about how the marks might actually have gotten there.

Art left me and went off, further back in the hall, to something he had missed or wished to examine further. And I? I began to walk down toward the gold plated grand piano Priscilla had made for Elvis as a birthday present. I approached with trepidation as the spiritual ambience began then to prevail upon my consciousness once more. As I expected, out of the silence came:

"There are others!"

This time chills fell over my body. I tried to ignore it. I turn to see a mini theater with a screen showing various performers of the Grand Ole Opry, doing a variety of famous numbers. At the back was a "pew" from the original home of the Opry, the Ryman Theater. I sat in this pew and reflected. I reasoned that there must be a lot of psychic energy connected with this pew. I swayed in and out of the ongoing show and the "otherworld," expecting more was to come.

Although, as I have said, and I repeat, I really believed I was just imagining things, because who was I to hear from Elvis? Why would Elvis want to speak to me?

"Okay, I'll bite––who?" I sent out into the mental ether.

"Johnny Cash."

"What? Johnny Cash is here too?"

Yes was the reply.

Whoa . . . Johnny Cash?

"There are others."

"Okay," I said. "Who else?"

"Patsy Cline."

"Yikes!" I could feel my pulse racing. If this wasn't real, then I need the men in white to come to take me away.

"There are others." Spoken matter-of-factly.

Now I realized my head was hurting and starting to spin. I was getting dizzy and even nauseated. In retrospect, the mental and physical drain was a further indication that this was a genuine spiritual encounter.

"No more, no more, this is as much as I can take for now." Real or not, I was flipping out from the anxiety. I got up from the pew, tried to clear my mind, and continued with the tour. Art caught up to me, we engaged in some conversation on the exhibits so far, and proceeded down to the second floor.

The second floor had a lot of interesting exhibits. What I most remember of the displays on this floor were clothing artists wore for memorable performances. There was an energy in the atmosphere that was hard to describe. As we followed exhibit after exhibit, I remarked to Art that there was a very "churchy" feeling to the museum. I noted that all that was missing was relics and holy water. I may have thrown this in as a humorous aside at this point, but I wasn't really kidding. Maybe the energy and miraculous quality of holy waters and relics are not so different from that imparted to the articles of world-renowned artists.

I sensed the presence of many, many country music spirits.

About halfway through the second floor, there was an entrance to a small theater where a film documentary on Tim McGraw and Faith Hill was repeating at regular intervals. We went in and sat down. The film began.

I tried watching, but my "company" would not release me, interjecting: "We are here." Elvis, Johnny, and Patsy in unison, it seemed.

"There are others!"

All right, I needed to clear up a few things with Elvis, Johnny, and Patsy.

"Look, telling me you are here—what am I supposed to do with this? I don't even know if this is real. Unless you can validate here in the real world that you really are here . . . telling me that you . . . and others . . . are here, what am I supped to do? I am not going to tell this to anyone ever, unless I have good validation to back me up. You have got to do something to validate this!"

I returned my attention to watching some of the film. A thought came to me. And I spoke mentally to the spirits. "Wait, I have it! Maybe, just maybe, if there are enough of you, you could get together and concentrate to get someone to do something unusual that would indeed validate this." I had an idea indeed. As there were not many visitors in attendance at the time, I had an idea for a validating experience.

Sometimes spirits can move objects, or put an idea into a person's mind to do something. If there were as many spirits present as Elvis was suggesting, then maybe they could do it.

"Concentrate on someone on the second floor, and try to get them to drop a penny. Actually, any coin will do. You have some time while this show finishes. So if before I leave this second floor I pick up a coin that someone has dropped, I will consider that I am truly in communication with the three of you—and others."

So setting this as the condition of validation, I was able to watch the rest of the show uninterrupted. When the show ended, we continued passing through the exhibits on the floor. Eventually we went around a bend, and came to a small hallway with a story, that I must confess, I didn't read—except, at the top, where it referred to "The Past is Hallowed Ground." I thought that yes, this whole place has a sense of spiritual opalescence.

This short hallway led to the Hall of Fame, where plaques of artists filled a large circular room. Between the hallway and this room, and to the left, we came upon a long staircase leading down to the first floor. I walked over to the banner to view the hall from this higher perspective.

There, right there, leaning on the railing, looking down, right under my nose, I saw a short waterfall leading into a stream that ran with the railing parallel with the stairwell.

In this stream . . . in this stream . . . filling this stream . . . from the pool where the waterfall began, all the way down to the first floor––were coins, coins, coins! Coins that people had dropped, dropped into the waters as they passed . . . many, many pennies! Other coins too, but mostly pennies. My hand, which was touching the water, reached in and pulled up a penny. I was in a state of shock, staring at the coin in my hand.

Not only did I have my validation, I had a sup validation! Obviously, I did not come up with the idea to look for coins. The spirits, knowing about the fountain that lay ahead, sent that idea to me. Maybe it too was clairaudient, but at the time too subtle for me to recognize.

I was lost in the awesomeness of the moment. It started to break as I heard Art asking, "Joan, are you all right? Are you all right? Joan, what's wrong? Are you all right?"

I may have left my body for a moment. This was indeed a transcendent experience. After an immeasurable time away, his voice began to pull me back. It was very hard for me to leave that place behind, but coaxed by him, I returned. Art had no idea what was going on. He isn't one for accepting paranormal experiences. On our way down to Nashville from Chicago, we had talked about the paranormal. He had shared with me his skepticism, as he had never had a personal experience. I owed him an explanation, however awkward it would be. The spirits had made their point. I had to tell him what I had just experienced. So saying, I am now sharing it with you.

In retrospection of this experience, I could only say "Of course!" Of course, it makes so much sense. My friend was a skeptic because he had never experienced a ghost anywhere. He had visited cemeteries, haunted houses, woods, and the like, and nothing. Many skeptics are so for these reasons. Well, there may just have not been any there; one has to go where they are. That's the place to start. They are most certainly at the Country Music Hall of Fame. Elvis made that clear to me. Perhaps this was the purpose of my encounter, to welcome you to come visit with them.

It makes sense that the spirit of the stars of country music would come to see the items that meant so much to them in life; to meet with one another and reminisce, to tour the exhibits and make note of new ones, to talk about current and past stars, and the like. As for lucky me––I got to tour with Elvis, Patsy, and John.

Bibliography

Books

Atwater, P. M. H. *We Live Forever: The Real Truth about Death*. Virginia: ARE Press, 2004.

Browne, Sylvia. *Book of Angels*. California: Hay House, 2003.

------. *Life on the Other Side*. New York: New American Library, 2000.

------. *The Other Side and Back*. California: Hay House, 2001.

Choquette, Sonia. *The Psychic Pathway*. New York: Three Rivers Press, 1994.

Cooper, Rabbi David. *Ecstatic Kabbalah*. Sounds True, 2005.

------. *God Is a Verb*. New York: Riverhead Books, 1997.

Goldman, Karen. *The Angel Book*. New York: Simon and Schuster, 1988.

Grant, Robert J. *The Place We Call Home: Exploring the Soul's Existence after Death*. Virginia: ARE Press, 2000.

Hoffman, Edward. *The Hebrew Alphabet*. Canada: San Francisco Chronical Books, 1998.

James, John and Frank Cherry. *The Grief Recovery Book*. New York: Harper Collins, 1988.

Rabbi Nachman of Breslov. *The Empty Chair.* Breslov Research Institute, 1994.

Sims, Darcie D. *Why Are All the Casseroles Tuna?* New Mexico: Big A and Company, 1992.

Van Praagh, James. *Healing Grief.* New York: New American Library, 2001.

------. *Meditations with James Van Praagh.* New York: Fireside, 2003.

------. *Unfinished Business.* New York: Harper One, 2009.

Virtue, Doreen, PhD. *Angels 101.* New York: Hay House, 2006.

------. *Chakra Clearing.* New York: Hay House, 1998.

------. *Healing with the Angels.* New York: Hay House, 1999

Audiotapes

Cooper, Rabbi David A. *Kabbalah Meditations*. Sounds True, 1995. Two-audiotape series.

------. *The Holy Chariot*. Sounds True, 1997. Six-audiotape series.

------. *The Mystical Kabbalah*. Sounds True, 1997. Five-audiotape series.

Moskowitz, Rabbi David. *Kabbalah: Life 101*. New York: The Kabbalah Learning Center, 2000. Five-audiotape series.

Zeller, David. *The Stories of Rebbe Nachman*. Sounds True, 1996. Six-audiotape series.

Videotapes

Kabbalah Learning Center. *Kabbalah*. California, 1999.

------. *The Power of Kabbalah*. California, 1998.

Edwards Brothers Malloy
Thorofare, NJ USA
March 10, 2015